Sacred
Privilege

Also by Kay Warren

Choose Joy

Choose Joy Devotional

Sacred Privilege

YOUR LIFE AND MINISTRY AS A PASTOR'S WIFE

KAY WARREN

Revell

a division of Baker Publishing Group
Grand Rapids, Michigan

© 2017 by Kay Warren

Published by Revell
a division of Baker Publishing Group
PO Box 6287, Grand Rapids, MI 49516-6287
www.revellbooks.com

Paperback edition published 2018
ISBN 978-0-8007-2967-7

Printed in the United States of America

The Library of Congress has cataloged the original edition as follows:
Names: Warren, Kay, 1954– author.
Title: Sacred privilege : the life and ministry of a pastor's wife / Kay Warren.
Description: Grand Rapids : Revell, 2017. | Includes bibliographical references.
Identifiers: LCCN 2016048340 | ISBN 9780800728168 (cloth)
Subjects: LCSH: Spouses of clergy. | Wives.
Classification: LCC BV4395 .W28 2017 | DDC 253/.22—dc23
LC record available at https://lccn.loc.gov/2016048340

Unless otherwise indicated, Scripture quotations are from the Holy Bible, New International Version®. NIV®. Copyright © 1973, 1978, 1984, 2011 by Biblica, Inc.™ Used by permission of Zondervan. All rights reserved worldwide. www.zondervan.com

Scripture quotations labeled AMP-CE are from the Amplified® Bible, copyright © 1954, 1958, 1962, 1964, 1965, 1987 by The Lockman Foundation. Used by permission. (www.Lockman.org)

Scripture quotations labeled CEV are from the Contemporary English Version © 1991, 1992, 1995 by American Bible Society. Used by permission.

Scripture quotations labeled GNT are from the Good News Translation—Second Edition. Copyright © 1992 by American Bible Society. Used by permission.

Scripture quotations labeled GW are from GOD'S WORD®. © 1995 God's Word to the Nations. Used by permission of Baker Publishing Group.

Scripture quotations labeled KJV are from the King James Version of the Bible.

Scripture quotations labeled Message are from THE MESSAGE. Copyright © by Eugene H. Peterson 1993, 1994, 1995, 1996, 2000, 2001, 2002. Used by permission of NavPress. All rights reserved. Represented by Tyndale House Publishers, Inc.

Scripture quotations labeled NASB are from the New American Standard Bible®, copyright © 1960, 1962, 1963, 1968, 1971, 1972, 1973, 1975, 1977, 1995 by The Lockman Foundation. Used by permission. (www.Lockman.org)

Scripture quotations labeled NCV are from the New Century Version®. Copyright © 2005 by Thomas Nelson, Inc. Used by permission. All rights reserved.

Scripture quotations labeled NLT are from the Holy Bible, New Living Translation, copyright © 1996, 2004, 2015 by Tyndale House Foundation. Used by permission of Tyndale House Publishers, Inc., Carol Stream, Illinois 60188. All rights reserved.

Scripture quotations labeled Phillips are from The New Testament in Modern English, revised edition—J. B. Phillips, translator. © J. B. Phillips 1958, 1960, 1972. Used by permission of Macmillan Publishing Co., Inc.

Scripture quotations labeled TLB are from The Living Bible, copyright © 1971. Used by permission of Tyndale House Publishers, Inc., Carol Stream, Illinois 60188. All rights reserved.

Scripture quotations labeled Voice are taken from The Voice™. Copyright © 2008 by Ecclesia Bible Society. Used by permission. All rights reserved.

18   19   20   21   22   23   24   7   6   5   4   3   2   1

To four pastors' wives whose lives inspire me . . .

Amy Warren Hilliker,
Bobbie Lawson Lewis,
Dorothy Armstrong Warren,
and Chaundel Warren Holladay

CONTENTS

A PERSONAL TRIBUTE
FROM RICK WARREN

Before you read this book, I want you to know

that none of my life's contributions would have happened

without Kay's enormous influence on me,

her *belief* in me,

her *prayers* for me,

her *grace* toward me,

her *advice* to me,

her *support* of me,

and her *partnership* with me.

Without Kay, there would have never

been a Saddleback Church,

there would be no Purpose Driven Life,

no Global PEACE Plan,

no Daily Hope Broadcast,

no Celebrate Recovery movement,

no Daniel Plan or Orphan Care Initiative,

no HIV&AIDS or All-Africa Initiatives,

no Purpose Driven Fellowship of Churches,

or any of the other ministries and tools

that Saddleback Church has brought to the world.

I've never known anyone more *committed*

to *courageously* facing personal faults and fears,

more determined to grow in *Christ* regardless of the cost,

and more *devoted* to treating everyone with dignity

than my wife.

She has made me a better man, husband, pastor, and leader.

And she is *amazing*.

"[Pastors], love your wives just as Christ loved the church."

Ephesians 5:25 (GNT)

PREFACE

When I began sharing this material with pastors' wives almost thirty years ago, I was young in ministry with plenty of questions and not a lot of answers. I titled my message "The Changing Role of the Pastor's Wife." As Saddleback grew and our ministry expanded, I changed it to "Growing with Your Church." Then life and ministry got pretty intense, which was reflected in the next title: "How to Keep the Ministry from Killing You!" Now at this point—after decades of serving God in ministry—I've realized it's best titled "Sacred Privilege: Your Life and Ministry as a Pastor's Wife."

If you and I could sit down and have a cup of tea together and you felt comfortable enough to be vulnerable, I wonder what you would tell me about being married to a pastor and your life in ministry. I wonder how you would title your own talk or book.

Many of you knew before you married that your husband was headed for the pastorate, but some of you did not see it coming! Your hubby was actively working in another career when

God called your family to radically shift direction and enter the ministry. Some of you are married to the senior or lead pastor, and some of you are married to a pastor in a staff position. Some of you are total newbies. You're recent church planters on your own, or you're helping to launch a video campus in a location separate from the "mother ship," or maybe you didn't grow up in a Christian home and absolutely everything about a life in ministry is still a mystery. Some of you are seasoned veterans. You've been at this for decades and might even be approaching retirement. You know ministry like the back of your hand. Others of you are smack dab in the middle; you're not newbies, but you're not near the finish line either. You've got a few years of experience under your belt—enough to have a pretty good feel for what life as a pastor's wife is going to be like for you.

Recently, I took a nonscientific survey of more than three thousand pastors' wives who follow me or Rick on social media and heard four distinct responses to questions about life in ministry. There is a group of you that is genuinely excited. You consider ministry a privilege and an honor, and you love your life as a woman married to a pastor. Yes, there are some real ups and downs, but there are more positives than negatives to living a life of full-time ministry, and overall, you'd choose it again.

Then there is a second group of you that is not quite as excited as the first group. The stresses and difficulties have made ministry challenging beyond what you were expecting, and honestly, the jury is out. You could go either way. If you stay in ministry, you know you'll survive, but if your husband decides to pursue another profession, you might be relieved.

Then there is a third smaller group. You have been broken by a life in full-time ministry. Your dreams are shattered; your patience with criticism, change, and financial struggle is long exhausted. Your family has taken "one for the team" one too many times. You constantly have to fight against bitterness and disillusionment taking over. When you look ahead to more years of living this way, you get a desperate sinking feeling in the pit of your stomach. Frankly, you are done.

There is yet another group of you that is deeply frustrated by the state of the Western church—angered by its silence or stance on injustice, racial reconciliation, poverty, sexuality, the environment, and any number of other social concerns—and you find yourself either emotionally or physically distancing yourself from church as you've known it.

I found myself nodding my head in understanding and empathy as I read the comments from thousands of my fellow pastors' wives. So much of what they said rang true in my heart. I could identify with the range of emotions and reactions. Their stories made sense to me; I've lived many of them myself. That's because ministry is the only life I know. No matter which way I turn, I am surrounded by the ministry. I'm a pastor's daughter and a pastor's wife. My daughter is married to a pastor. My sister-in-law is married to a pastor. My nephew is a pastor. My niece is married to a pastor. Three of my grandchildren are growing up in a pastor's home. My son is the president of a ministry that serves pastors. Starting with my birth and continuing for six decades, ministry has defined my existence. That means I am intimately acquainted with the world of the local church and the people who populate it—the good, the bad, and the ugly. I've known some of the truly great Christians in ministry—simple men and women who bravely, repeatedly, and sacrificially serve Jesus with every fiber of their being. I've witnessed the scandals and exposés of those in highly visible ministries as well as the mistakes and sins that never reached the public eye. I think I've seen it all in more than forty years in ministry, and I still say it's been a sacred privilege to give my life in full-time ministry.

As you read, you need to know my bias. I love the church of Jesus Christ—I mean I *really* love the beauty, the promise, and the potential of the church. To be honest, my love and respect for the church have waxed and waned over the years. At different moments, I've been disgusted with the church and some of its scandals; hated the injustices and prejudices; been embarrassed by the failures of highly visible leaders; and been completely frustrated by tunnel vision, small thinking, and petty arguments over what color to paint the church kitchen while the world around us goes to hell in a handbasket. At the end of the day, though, I have learned to genuinely admire God's brilliance in creating an entity called "the church"—the *only place on earth* where eternal souls are meant to find salvation and safe harbor; sacrificial servanthood is routinely practiced; cultural, racial, economic, gender, and ethnic differences are abolished; and true oneness and unity can occur.

My goal is not to write the quintessential book for pastors' wives—the one and only book you'll ever need as you navigate the tumultuous, often murky waters of ministry. This is not a one-size-fits-all book of advice because I don't pretend to speak for every pastor's wife! Pastors' spouses come in every variety, size, and shape imaginable—some are men! Over the decades of my ministry, the role of women married to pastors, as well as of women in general, has radically evolved. From behind-the-scenes, mostly-in-the-home pastors' wives of my mother's generation to women copastoring or serving as the senior pastor—as well as everything in between—the role of the pastor's wife has not remained static.

That means every generation has to adapt to a changing culture and contextualize ministry—and that includes books about serving in ministry. Some of the pastors' wives' books that informed and inspired me forty years ago are ridiculously out of date. No young pastor's wife today could read them without laughing at instructions to keep cans of tuna on hand for a quick tuna noodle casserole when church members drop by unexpectedly at dinnertime. Or advice about the amount of makeup to wear or the admonition to wear simple jewelry and dark colors.

Though times and our culture change, I do believe there are some timeless lessons to offer—lessons I learned first as a pastor's daughter, then as a youth pastor's wife, a church planter's wife, and eventually a lead pastor's wife. I want to pass on the hard-won truths, the foundational principles, the anchors for your soul, the survival techniques, the never-forget certainties that will keep you steady and stable, even joyful, on the journey. Maybe I can save you from a few mistakes, point you in a healthy direction, give you comfort and solace when the bottom falls out, and help you make the most of the time God has allotted to you. My experiences will resonate with some of you—"Yes, that's the way it is for me!"—but some of you may say, "That doesn't fit my situation at all." That's okay.

One last thought as you start to read. This is not a book from a perfect woman telling you about her perfect life. I intend to be *really* honest—sometimes uncomfortably so. My biggest complaint about books written for pastors or pastors' wives is that they're not honest enough about how hard a life in ministry can be; the challenges our marriages and families face; or the internal struggles, wrestling, anxieties, and doubts that can occur. I will be as direct, raw, and transparent as I can without crossing into inappropriate sharing. You might disagree with what I consider appropriate sharing. I certainly don't want to dishonor my parents, my husband, my kids, or my church by what I share. Please know that my intent is to reflect the range of emotions and reactions I have experienced. You might be experiencing some of the same emotions, and I hope to create an atmosphere of acceptance and safety for you as you read. I want you to know you're not alone. Most of all, I'm praying you'll find a few timeless nuggets of encouragement and hope that strengthen you as you serve Jesus and his church and that you will see yourself as a person who has been given a sacred privilege.

1

The Story of a Church Girl

I'm a church girl. I've always been a church girl.

I have the faded nursery enrollment certificate from my dad's church given to me when I was one week old to prove it. Most of my earliest memories are tied to the people and the small churches my dad pastored in San Diego, California. I've proudly marched into the sanctuary carrying the Christian flag to the tune of "Onward Christian Soldiers" during many a Vacation Bible School. I've fallen asleep on a hard, wooden pew while my father or a visiting evangelist preached his heart out every night at a two-week revival. I learned the books of the Bible when I was eight and could find Obadiah faster than any of my friends. I studied and memorized dozens of verses to become a "queen" in Girls Auxiliary (Southern Baptist's version of Girl Scouts). I became the church pianist at twelve. I've been to hundreds of potlucks and Wednesday night suppers where I've eaten mountains of cold fried chicken, inhaled bowl after bowl of homemade ice cream on hot summer nights at after-church fellowships, and drank more red Kool-Aid than is good for any human being.

I remember feeling the pressure to be the perfect pastor's kid who knew all the right answers to Bible trivia questions. I recall the heavy pressure to be a model for other people and especially the pressure not to embarrass or cause shame to my parents by exposing our family flaws. I also remember being confused by the people who told me I *had* to do something because I was the pastor's daughter and those who told me I *couldn't* do something because I was the pastor's daughter. It often seemed as if I couldn't win.

Many of my experiences are probably common to others who grew up in a pastor's home, but a few incidents weren't related to my dad's job per se, and they marked me in ways that have taken me years to overcome.

I can't remember a time when I didn't feel like the weight of the world was on my shoulders. From a very young age I was a serious, sensitive child who felt things deeper and differently than my peers. In my teen years, it seemed as if there was a "switch" inside of me, and my mood could flip from happy to sad in an instant, often over very trivial things. Even after I got married, there would be periods of time that we called my "existential angst"—days when nothing mattered, everything looked bleak, and my energy level was extremely low. It always passed, and within a short time, I was back to feeling like myself. Now I recognize the signs of low level depression, but that was not a word in my vocabulary at the time, and even if someone had suggested it, I would have dismissed it as nonsense. I was a Christian! Christians didn't get depressed.

I was molested by the son of the church janitor when I was four or five. I remember not telling my parents because it was "bad" and because as a young child I didn't have the language to express what had happened. This became my first secret.

Another confusing family secret was my dad had been divorced before he met my mother and I had a half-sister. His previous marriage and the existence of another child were forbidden topics—off-limits for discussion in our family and certainly not shared with other church members. Because I knew that I needed to help protect my dad from people who wouldn't understand his reasons for getting divorced, I carefully monitored my words and what I revealed about our family to others.

As a teenager, I felt very bold and adventurous one night at a neighbor's house where I was babysitting. I noticed a bottle of wine in their refrigerator and convinced myself that one sip wasn't going to hurt anybody—it wasn't going to send me to hell. With shaking hands and a racing heart, I took a sip. Instantly, I was convinced I was the worst sinner on the planet. I spat it out as fast as I could, washing my mouth out over and over again, terrified that my parents would be able to smell it on me after my one tiny sip. For those of you raised with a more tolerant view of Christians and alcohol (drinking but not drunkenness), this must seem like utter stupidity and silliness, but for me and my very sheltered upbringing, this qualified as downright rebellion! The pastor's daughter had another embarrassing secret.

If the one sip of wine left me feeling like a horrible rebel, my view of myself was about to sink even lower. The deepest place of confusion and internal struggle for me as a teenager was finding pornography at the home of these same neighbors where I babysat. I saw it on the end table next to their couch (yeah, they left it out) and was both fascinated and repelled by this forbidden material. Remember the time period—no internet, no cell phones, no instant availability of pornography, no private ability to obtain and peruse it 24/7. It mostly existed in magazine form, and I had never seen it before, not even in a store magazine rack. It was clearly taboo for a Christian young woman who sincerely wanted to live a pure and holy life for Jesus, but somehow one night I picked it up and looked at it. Instant self-loathing, guilt, and remorse. "How can I look at pornography? I love Jesus! I want to be a missionary! I'll never look at it again," I told myself. And I didn't. Until the next time I babysat. And the time after that. And the time after that. And before long, I was hooked. The good girl who loved Jesus with all her heart had a secret fascination with pornography, and the shame about killed me.

Again, given the time period, pornography wasn't always staring me in the face. But I would occasionally stumble upon it, and when I did, the cycle of temptation, giving in, shame, and remorse would repeat itself. I couldn't reconcile my temptations and my faith; I was torn apart on the inside. Worst of all, I couldn't tell anyone about it—no one. How could I possibly confess my weakness and repeated sin to a fellow Christian? I never even considered telling my parents, and the thought of unburdening myself to a friend or an older adult was simply not an option. Off the table. And so I continued in this state of internal conflict and failure, all the while knowing I was in deep trouble. I wanted out but didn't have a clue how to change.

Then I met Rick Warren when I was seventeen at a training to be part of a summer youth evangelism team that would travel to Baptist churches in the cities and towns of California. I distinctly remember being unimpressed (sorry, honey). To be fair, he felt the same way about me. He was a loud, guitar-playing, over-the-top extrovert who sucked the oxygen out of every room he entered, and his humor and passionate preaching soon drew many to him. I, on the other hand, was shy and reserved and way too in touch with my female adolescent emotions to appeal to a larger-than-life person like Rick.

But then we reconnected a year later as freshmen at California Baptist College, a small liberal arts college in Riverside, California, and became casual friends. Everybody knew him on our campus of six hundred students, and he quickly became a respected Christian leader, while I kept a lower profile, loving Jesus, college, the singing group I was a part of, and close girlfriends. Later our freshman year I began dating a really nice guy, but the relationship ended within a few months. I thought my heart was irreparably broken. To make a long story short, Rick tells me that a month before this guy broke up with me, Rick had an impression from the Lord: "You're going to marry Kay Lewis." He says he immediately dismissed it because (1) I was dating someone else and (2) he wasn't romantically interested in me. But when he walked around a corner at school one day, I nearly ran into him, and he says Cupid's arrow pierced his heart in a flash and he fell madly in love with me. So cute, huh? I was clueless. I had absolutely no idea about his newfound interest in me, but suddenly this Rick Warren guy—the guy who once told a friend that he didn't date because he didn't see why he should waste money on a girl he wasn't going to marry, and besides, God would point out the right girl and he would know—started sitting down next to me in the college cafeteria and engaging me in conversation. I immediately panicked because I had heard of his "not wasting money on a girl he wasn't going to marry" approach to romance. So why was he acting interested in me? I wasn't interested in him or any guy. I was still recovering from a painful breakup. I just hoped he would go away.

Within a few days of his sudden interest in me, he asked me out to Farrell's Ice Cream Parlour in the fall of 1973, and I grudgingly went. He made me nervous. He was nice to me and very attentive, but I just wasn't interested. A week later—eight days to be precise—he accompanied me to a revival meeting in a neighboring city where I was playing the piano. When we got back to campus, we prayed together to close out the evening. Sitting in the dark, I heard him say, "Will you marry me?" I was aghast. "What did you say?" Stammering now, he said, "I love you. Will you marry me?" Clearly the poor boy was delusional. Marry him? What in the world was the matter with him? But I recall instantly praying and asking the Lord what I should do. "I don't love him! I don't even really know him! I love someone else!" I heard God respond, "Say yes. I'll bring the feelings." And so with my nineteen-year-old understanding of life, romance, God, his will, faith, and my desire to be obedient to him, I said yes. Kay Lewis and Rick Warren got engaged.

We didn't tell anyone—least of all our families—because somewhere in the goofy brains of two nineteen-year-olds we knew it wasn't going to go over well, even at our Christian college, where "being led by the Spirit" had high value. So our engagement became our secret for the next six months.

Unfortunately, for Rick, I was a mess inside—talk about conflicted emotions. I knew I had heard God's voice when he told me to say yes to Rick's proposal, but those promised feelings of love and romance didn't show up. I continued to struggle with my feelings for the other guy and my lack of feelings for Rick. I felt so guilty—I knew I was hurting Rick by my on-again, off-again emotional response to him—but I felt trapped by what I understood God's will to be. Rick finally said he was going to end our engagement because I was breaking his heart. When I got myself straightened out and knew what I wanted, perhaps we could get back together.

After a month of separation, I realized that whether or not I had the romantic feelings I thought I should be feeling, Rick was the man I was supposed to marry. We got officially engaged this time around, complete with a simple diamond ring. No one knew that I remained baffled by the way God had led us to become engaged. To our friends and family, it seemed like a romantic story that was almost biblical—you know, like Isaac and Rebekah.

Rick immediately moved to Nagasaki, Japan, as a summer missionary to teach English, and I moved to Birmingham, Alabama, to work in the inner city for the summer. We faithfully wrote letters to each other that summer, but they always seemed to cross in the mail, so we were out of sync the entire time. Making a phone call was impossible—way too expensive to call internationally—and we had no cell phones, FaceTime, Skype, Facebook, Instagram, Twitter, or any other fantastic method of staying in touch. So we left each other at the beginning of the summer as mostly strangers, returned home as mostly strangers, and compounded the distance and unfamiliarity between us by living in different cities for the next year. When we did have a rare weekend together, we certainly didn't waste one precious minute on conflict or conflict resolution. Everything we should have talked about and learned to deal with was swept under the relationship carpet, where it waited, ready to pounce on us as soon as these two near-strangers said "I do" on June 21, 1975.

I stood in the foyer of First Baptist Church of Norwalk, California, where Rick was the youth pastor, anxiously clutching my daddy's arm, frightened by the numbness and confusion inside me. But as I walked down the aisle and stared into the shining eyes of the earnest, kind young man who had asked me to marry him, I knew I was loved. Passionately. Intensely. With a "till death do us part" kind of love. The way he looked at me on our wedding day became an anchor I would hold on to during the darker times when I wasn't sure we were going to survive the mess our marriage had become.

Our brand-new marriage took an instant nosedive. We didn't even make it to the end of our two-week honeymoon to British Columbia before we knew our relationship was in serious trouble. We had been warned about five areas of potential conflict all couples have to deal with, and we immediately jumped into all five of them: sex, communication, money, children, and in-laws. Nothing worked for us. Nothing. We were so young—barely twenty-one—and inexperienced, and when sex didn't work and we argued about sex, and then argued about our arguments and began to layer resentment on top of resentment, it was a perfect setup for misery and disenchantment. I had told Rick about being molested as a little girl—he was the first person I ever told—but because I was so unemotional about it, he figured it wasn't that significant an incident to me and basically forgot about it. I kept my occasional ventures into pornography a complete secret. How could I share that shame with a man I barely knew? So between the effects of the unaddressed molestation, the resulting brokenness in my sexuality, and the off-and-on pornography fascination, it shouldn't have been a surprise that sex didn't work.

What made it worse was that everyone considered us the perfect couple. We were both on fire for Jesus, had this romantic "God told me to marry you" story, were committed to God and the church, wanted to be missionaries or at least in full-time ministry—I mean, we marched down the aisle to the old hymn "To God Be the Glory." What else did we need for a happy, successful marriage?

Clearly, we needed more than what we started with. And when we returned from the honeymoon, already miserable and shocked at the depth of our unhappiness, we felt like we had nowhere to go with our wretched pain and marital failures. Our senior pastor and his wife were very kind to us, but there was no way we were going to confess to them that we were a mess right out of the gate. We thought everyone would be so disappointed in us and judge us as terrible Christians, unfit to lead. Maybe in some ways we were unfit to lead, but even that thought was terrifying.

> Maybe in some ways we were unfit to *lead*, but even that thought was *terrifying*.

Rick and I managed to limp our way through our first year of marriage, all the while he was a youth pastor to a vibrant group of kids who filled our small apartment at all hours of the day and night. We were young enough and naïve enough— and thoroughly conditioned by our strict upbringing—to not recognize the damage we were causing to ourselves by hiding and pretending everything was okay. We didn't get that we were living a lie. Well, maybe we understood it at some level, but we were too scared to bring it all out into the open. About a year and a half into our marriage, with tremendous shame and embarrassment, we sought counseling from a Christian psychologist, and his gracious words to us got us talking, although nothing was fixed.

On our second wedding anniversary, we moved to Fort Worth, Texas, for Rick to pursue a master's degree in theology so that he could become a senior pastor. We still had massive problems with sex, communication, and money, and we were in marital hell. The common understanding of the day was if you love Jesus enough, your marriage will be happy. What was so confusing was that we loved Jesus with all our hearts and were committed to the local church. How could things be so bad? The irony that Rick wanted to be a pastor but had a cruddy marriage wasn't wasted on us. The fact that we were miserable weighed on both of us like a giant boulder, but we didn't see any way out. I think we hoped that one morning we would just wake up and find it was all a bad dream and that somehow all our problems would simply vanish. I think they call that magical thinking. We wanted to honor the sacred wedding vows we had made before God and our loved ones, so divorce wasn't on our radar. But neither could we visualize living in such pain for the rest of our lives. We just didn't know what to do or how to create a healthy marriage out of the shattered pieces of conflict, disappointment, dysfunction, and resentment.

As part of his degree program, Rick was required to attend weekly group counseling sessions for a period of time. He didn't feel he could expose our brokenness to these fellow theology students, so he would fake it during the group sessions and come home so sick to his stomach he wanted to throw up. He grew increasingly angry about our secretly failing relationship, and with that suppressed anger came intense depression and anxiety.

While Rick was a full-time student, he spent many weekends traveling around the South speaking at churches and small conferences. I was working full-time and was the main breadwinner. I was the assistant to one of the VPs of the company, and my desk faced the elevator where everyone entered and exited throughout the day. It didn't take long for me to discover that a really good-looking guy worked on the same floor, and before I knew what was happening, I had spun a complete fantasy life in my head around this guy. I found "reasons" to take my lunch at the same time he did in the corporate lunchroom. There were "reasons" to walk by his office several times a day and smile and give a friendly wave. I sat at my desk and daydreamed about what it would be like to be in a relationship with him. I got nervous and my hands perspired when he talked to me. It was bad. Really, really bad. I detached my emotions from my husband and attached them to this guy who hardly even knew I existed. One day the emotional bubble burst when I walked by his office and heard him berating his wife on the phone. He was so rude and mean and ugly to her that I was completely shocked. It turned out my fantasy guy was a jerk. My ridiculous obsession with him ended in that moment because I caught a glimpse of the real man behind the good looks and didn't like what I saw.

But what if my emotional and physical attraction to him had been met with a corresponding attraction to me? What if he had entertained a similar fantasy? What if he had been receptive to my flirtatious behavior? What if he had been willing to jeopardize his family life for a silly, naïve young woman who was unhappy in her marriage? What if my actions had ended up putting me in the position of choosing between my marriage and an affair? The story could have had a very different ending. I could have lost my marriage. Yes, it was a bad marriage, but my fantasies didn't negate the fact that I had taken vows. Vows of faithfulness. Vows of love. Vows of lifelong commitment. Those vows didn't become null and void just because we didn't know how to love each other well. If I had abandoned my vows, my history would be different. I would have missed out on the rich, satisfying marriage that was still ahead of me, born out of the long and painful journey. I would have short-circuited the lessons learned along the way about self-centeredness, fear of vulnerability, broken self-identity, messed-up conflict management, and poor communication skills. I would have missed the joy of being a mother to Amy, Joshua, and Matthew. I would have missed being Grammy to Kaylie, Cassidy, Caleb, Cole, and Claire. I would have missed being a part of cofounding Saddleback Church, the most wonderful church on the planet. I would have missed out on becoming a global advocate for people living with HIV and for orphans and vulnerable children. I would have missed the chance to speak up for people living with mental illness, for suicide awareness and prevention. I would have forfeited the right to call the church to action on behalf of anyone living on the edges, the margins, outside the warmth of the fellowship of Jesus. I nearly lost everything I was dreaming of and longing for when I put my marriage at risk.

Through my decades of ministry, I've talked to hundreds of women and couples who were in lonely, unfulfilling marriages—marriages in which their dreams had turned to dust. Where the passion had long since been buried under the daily grind of careers, children, pressure, stress, and unfulfilled longings. Some of these marriages ended with a loud bang as anger and bitterness corroded any sense of decency and humanity and compassion for the other. Some ended with shock, soul-shattering pain, and disillusionment as betrayal made a mockery of the vows of faithfulness. Some ended with a thud; the unending battle for a healthy relationship free from addiction finally beat one partner to a pulp and he or she was just done and no longer willing to keep trying. Some ended with a quiet whisper—silence—as boredom, illness, financial struggles, or any other of myriad issues made even dry, brown grass on the other side of the fence look so much greener than the barren wasteland on their side of the fence.

I nearly lost *everything* I was dreaming of and longing for when I put my marriage at risk.

I hear you. I really do. I don't approach this subject from the Hallmark-card-version of marriage but from the blood, sweat, and tears of the trenches where our marriage was forged and is sustained. I know what it's like to choose to build our relationship; to seek marriage counseling again and again; to allow our small group and our family into the struggle; to determine one more time to say, "Let's start over" and "Please forgive me, I was wrong" and "I forgive you"; to admit that my way isn't the only way to see the world and to try to imagine what it's like to be on the other side of me; to choose to focus on what is good and right and honorable in my husband instead of what drives me crazy; to turn attraction to another man into attraction to my husband; to have vastly opposing opinions on how to handle and cope with a mentally ill child; to have fear and anxiety and panic threaten to swallow up normal life; to become consumed with the needs of one member of the family; to be cracked open by catastrophic grief and to share it with your spouse when you're so different; to figure out how to grieve and mourn together when your mentally ill child takes his life in a violent way and your grief is public because you're in ministry and your glass-house, fishbowl existence is fodder for scrolling headlines on CNN. I don't know your exact circumstances, but I know mine, and to say marriage has been hard is as severe an understatement as I can muster up.

Yet, it's also been the very best thing that has ever happened to either of us. We wouldn't be who we are today without each other. I'm a better Christian, a better woman, a better mother, a better friend, and a better minister because of Rick. He says he's a better Christian, a better man, a better father, a better friend, and a better minister because of me. The shrieks of iron sharpening iron have often sounded like gears grinding on bare metal, but the result has been profound personal growth in both of us. He is my best friend. Forever. Our song used to be "Happy to Be Stuck with You" by Huey Lewis and the News because it spoke of the realities of our life together. It acknowledged the poor fit between us, the conflict, the struggle, the desire to be in an easier relationship but also the choice we had made to stay together because we had come to peace about our differences and learned how to really love each other. But we've chosen a new song—one that more accurately reflects the passion we feel for each other. Gladys Knight's rendition of "You're the Best Thing That Ever Happened to Me" turns us sappy and weepy and googly-eyed like we never were at twenty-one. Why?

We've beaten the odds that divorce would be the outcome of our ill-advised union. We've weathered my breast cancer and melanoma. We've survived the mental illness and suicide of our son Matthew. And now we *know*. We know we are the best thing that has ever happened to each other. I am in love with the man God brought into my life so many years ago. Each of us is not who the other was looking for, but each of us is who the other desperately needed to become the person we each are today.

There's so much more, but I'll save it for later chapters. At the end of the day, the most important thing is for you to know we're all on the same journey, all holders of the same sacred privilege. You need to embrace your own story—all of it—for the glory of God and the growth of his kingdom.

Sharing the Dream

But my God lives; and he has my heart.

SARAH EDWARDS,
wife of Jonathan Edwards

When I was in college, I spent a summer serving in several inner-city churches in another state. After a few weeks, it dawned on me that I never saw the pastor's wife at one of the churches. I asked if she was okay and was told, "Oh, she doesn't come. She doesn't want her husband to be a pastor; she attends maybe once every three or four months." You could drive by their house on any day of the week and find her car in front of the house, where she was with her small children. I'm not criticizing this woman. I didn't know this couple or the backstory of their marriage or ministry. All I know is they left ministry shortly after.

Over the course of a lifetime, I've had the opportunity to meet hundreds of diverse ministry couples—each as unique and individual as the men and women themselves. Some of these couples struggled their entire ministry to be in sync with each other, while others eventually figured out a rhythm that allowed each to flourish and thrive. Many variables have to be factored in when you try to nail down the traits or habits that might predict which couples will last in ministry. But I've noticed one common trait in couples who thrive over the long haul: the ability to see themselves as a team who shares a God-given dream. I believe this one factor can actually make or break the ministry God has called you to. Being a team sharing a dream can revitalize a marriage, a family, a local church, and ultimately the kingdom of God.

When Rick was in seminary at Southwestern Baptist Theological Seminary in Fort Worth, Texas, he surprised me one day with a request. "Honey, this summer I'd like for you to go with me to a church growth conference in Southern California. I'm interested in planting a church."

My response was less than enthusiastic or supportive. "Uh, thanks, but no thanks. Why in the world would I ever want to attend a church growth conference? And what's this about planting a church? I thought you were going to be a pastor of an established church."

I objected to his idea on every level. I wasn't interested in church planting, we didn't have the money to make the trip or pay the conference fees, I couldn't take the time off work, and it made me anxious to think about planting a church—the part about no money, no building, no members, no security or stability bothered me.

He outsmarted me at every turn. He said, "We'll do it cheap and fast—we'll drive straight through so we don't have motel bills. I'll request scholarships for us. We'll stay with your parents so you can see your family. And we can go to the beach!" Since we were dirt poor and could barely afford to make long-distance calls, he wore down my resistance by dangling in front of me the chance to see my parents and younger brother. The chance to visit my beloved Southern California coast was the final incentive. Still, I pretty much went kicking and screaming to the church growth conference. We read Karen Burton Mains's book *Open Heart, Open Home* aloud to each other to pass the time, but I also remember the tension between us during that 1,388-mile drive.

Have you ever had one of those experiences when your life is positively changed forever? When your well-laid plans suddenly explode into a vapor and the future opens up before you in such wonder that it takes your breath away?

That's what happened to me at the church growth conference. In each session, I listened to speakers challenging us to keep the uninterested, unchurched community in mind as we contemplated ways to catch their attention long enough to let them know God loved them. Their words began to peel the layers of opposition away from my frightened, resistant heart. Bit by bit, a word at a time, the dream that had sprouted in Rick's heart began to take root in mine as I caught the vision of reaching unchurched people for Jesus Christ. My fond imaginings of security and stability evaporated with barely a backward glance. Even now I choke up writing these words, my mind's eye recapturing the almost uncontainable hope of partnering with God in a new and fresh way that could potentially change the eternal destiny of thousands of people.

Yes, I got to visit briefly with my family, and yes, I got to breathe in the salty beach air that I missed, but most of that has faded from my thoughts. What stands out in bold relief is the drive back to Fort Worth—the two of us chattering and talking over each other as I attempted to write down our ideas on random pieces of paper while Rick drove. We were twenty-four-year-old dreamers with wildly beating hearts, almost overwhelmed by the dream of planting a church for people who didn't even know God loved them. In the 1,388 miles back to Fort Worth, we became a team, sharing a dream for the glory of God. Little did we know how God would use that experience to change *everything* we had envisioned for our lives.

Ephesians 2:10 says, "For we are God's masterpiece. He has created us anew in Christ Jesus, so we can do the good things he planned for us long ago" (NLT). This affirms to me that long before Rick and I were born God knew we would marry and planned very specific things for us to do in our life together in ministry. The dreams we were dreaming didn't originate with us but with him.

> But when we began to share the *dream*—when it became *our* dream—we began to think more about what we could accomplish *together* than we could individually.

Up to that point, I often felt like I was a useless appendage hanging at Rick's side as he went about his speaking ministry. I saw myself as a tag-along person few noticed. It didn't help things much that he was used to traveling and doing ministry as a single guy; it took him a while to adjust to being married. When he spoke at youth revivals or preached in churches, he didn't even always remember to introduce me from the pulpit. He tried hard, though, and wrote in big letters on the top of his sermon notes INTRODUCE KAY!

But when we began to share the dream—when it became *our* dream—we began to think more about what we could accomplish together than we could individually. The truth of Ecclesiastes 4:9–12—that two are better than one—began to sink in.

Two people are better off than one, for they can help each other succeed. If one person falls, the other can reach out and help. But someone who falls alone is in real trouble. Likewise, two people lying close together can keep each other warm. But how can one be warm alone? A person standing alone can be attacked and defeated, but two can stand back-to-back and conquer. Three are even better, for a triple-braided cord is not easily broken. (NLT)

We caught a glimpse of how our individual gifts and talents, when united in purpose and direction, could make us powerful partners together in ministry.

— See Yourselves as a Team —

The word *team* comes from the Old English and referred to a set of draft animals yoked together. A more modern definition expands on the concept by adding "a number of people who act together as a group, either in a sport or in order to achieve something."[1] Rick defines a team as two or more people who have common goals and also deep communication about those goals. You and your husband may be working together, but if you're not communicating clearly on a deep level, you're really not a team. Likewise, you may be communicating with each other on a deep level, but if you have different goals, you're not a team. "Team" means having common goals for your ministry as well as deep communication about those goals.

As I said in the preface, the role of a pastor's wife varies widely and no single model fits all of us. But I've noticed three common models of ministry couples (with multiple variations on these basic models): share everything, share much, or share little.

First, there are couples who share everything. The husband and wife are copastors. They have the same title and share not only the dream and the vision but also similar responsibilities and perhaps even salaries. A second model is a couple who shares much. The husband is the pastor and the wife may or may not have an official title, but she actively serves and leads, shares the vision and the dream, has influence with her husband, and is respected by other leaders in the church. A third, fairly traditional model is a couple who shares little. In this model, the husband has much greater responsibility than the wife. He (or the church) may have a fairly firm set of expectations for her, but her responsibilities come with little authority. The wife is present and involved, but she does not have much of a voice when it comes to making decisions. Regardless of which of these three models you fit into, the concept of being a team has more to do with intangibles than with a chart or title; it's more about attitude than about tasks and job descriptions.

There's a strong biblical basis for seeing yourselves as a team who shares a dream. It's called being "one flesh." This term was first used in Genesis 2:24 to describe the union of Adam and Eve: two separate and distinct bodies physically joined in such a way as to appear as one person. Nothing else even comes close to demonstrating God's desire for a husband and a wife to be united and harmonious than the physical act of becoming one flesh. And yet we all know couples who would say that while the sexual aspect of their marriage is strong, they find it difficult to get along outside of the bedroom. They lead largely separate lives, headed in different directions with little to cement the feelings of oneness. Their emotional and spiritual oneness is fractured, leaving both unsatisfied and longing for greater intimacy. That's why physical oneness is meant to represent a deeper bond, not just the physical ability to mesh body parts but a spiritual and emotional unity and harmony that lend meaning to the physical.

I want to be as one flesh physically, emotionally, and spiritually as is possible with Rick, and that goal has pushed me to become a part of his world.

—— A Part of His World ——

At a time when having small children and doing my best to keep up with their needs and demands prevented me from being as active in ministry as I desired, Rick and I felt emotionally distant from each other. Nothing was actively wrong, but we were like ships passing in the night, each of us busy with our individual responsibilities. The "sharing the dream and being part of a team" strategy we started the church with began to fade a bit as life circumstances propelled us into a different season. I didn't know much about what was happening in his world, and he didn't know much about what was happening in mine. During one of our intense conversations about our mutual frustration, Rick tentatively posed a question he had read in a marriage book: Is it true that the more a woman chooses to make herself a part of her husband's world the more he will choose to be a part of her world?

I was riveted by that question and pondered it for days. I'm not going to wade into a conversation about whose turn it was to make the first move—which of us needed to try to be a part of whose world first. That kind of me-first thinking can become a distraction and is what dooms too many relationships to disappointment and bitterness.

Many times I've had to choose between "me first" and "the marriage first." Rick could easily tell you about the times he has set aside "me first" and put his energy into building our relationship. That's the mutuality spoken of in Ephesians 5:21–33. In my less-than-holy moments, though, I've found myself holding out for Rick to initiate something in our relationship on my timetable and in the way I want him to do it. I've played that game, and no one wins. I'm learning to put my energy into what it is I ultimately want—for us to be a part of each other's world. On the occasion he raised the question about a wife becoming a part of her husband's world, I decided that if I needed to make the first move, then so be it. It became obvious to me that if I wanted him to be a part of *my* world, I would have to do whatever I could to be a part of *his* world. There were some deliberate decisions I needed to make.

In seminary, when Rick began talking church planting, church health, demographics, charts, and trends, he might as well have been speaking to me in ancient Babylonian. Blah, blah, blah, blah, blah, blah, blah. On top of that, I didn't really care to know! While Rick is still the church health expert, I know a lot more today than I did when we first began. The reason I do is because I have chosen to read some of the books he reads, listen to the sermons he listens to, and attend some of the conferences he attends. If you want to be a part of your husband's world and his ministry on a level beyond the basics—on a level where you're sharing ideas and dreams—then you need to make the effort to enter his world.

This might seem unfair—and you might have a laundry list of why this simply isn't possible for you and why it's your husband's turn to make a move in your direction—but protesting that it's not fair won't get you to where you really want to be: in a place of oneness, harmony, and unity. Instead, why not ask him some simple questions: "What are the two most influential books you've read in the last six months? Is there a sermon podcast that really touched your heart recently?" When he picks himself up off the floor, be ready to write down the titles. If you sense receptivity to your attempt to connect on a deeper level, you might say something like, "I know we haven't shared this before (or in a while), but it's very important to me. I'd really like to hear your dreams and hopes for the church in the next six months."

There aren't many men who will reject a wife's *sincere* interest in the things that interest them. Why? Because it says, "I value you. I want to be a part of your world. I want to know what you care about. I want to know what means something to you." Your husband probably wants to share but may not know how to. Maybe he's just gotten used to the two of you being absorbed in your own responsibilities and the emotional disconnect hasn't registered with him yet. See if he won't gradually invite you more and more into that part of his heart as you show genuine curiosity for what's on his mind. Take note

I said "sincere interest" and "genuine curiosity." Becoming one flesh is not about manipulation or pretending or faking it to get something for yourself. It's about taking each other into your heart of hearts.

I'd also suggest, when possible, attending the same conferences he does or at least watching them online. There is a massive relational difference between attending a meaningful event together and hearing about it after the fact. Think of a time you went to a women's retreat and came home so excited, and he said, "How was the retreat?" You replied, "Oh, it was just so inspirational!" Maybe he said, "Well, tell me about it," and so you tried to tell him why it meant so much to you, and within seconds you saw his eyes glaze over and he muttered, "Yeah, okay. Yeah," and you started getting frustrated. "Don't you get it? It was really awesome!" and he said, "Well, I'm trying," and you both gave up. But later that week you saw some of the other women who went on the retreat, and you all just started jabbering back and forth with excitement, enthusiasm, and shared memories. "Remember when she said this, and how much it meant?" You could have talked for hours with the women who were with you at the retreat.

What's the difference? The difference is you and the other women shared a relational and spiritual experience that your husband did not. When you attend conferences or events together as a couple, you increase the odds that it will build your marriage and deepen your relationship because of the shared experiences you can process together. I can't encourage this enough!

A bit of a side note: it's a well-known fact that when people share common goals, they're drawn closer together. This is partially why pastors and their secretaries or pastors and their staff members are susceptible to affairs. When people work together for a common goal and they're communicating on a deep level about those goals, it's natural for emotional bonds to build. We'll talk more about this later, but at the end of the day, none of us want our spouse to develop more closeness with a co-worker than with us.

If you feel isolated from the ministry you and your husband are engaged in and wish he would talk or share more deeply with you, do what you can to make yourself a part of his world. Hopefully, he will respond to your sincere desire for intimacy and will, in turn, have an interest and a desire to be in your world.

There are no ironclad guarantees, of course—this is not always an A + B = C world. The fact is some men have a hard time sharing on a deep and intimate level with anyone, let alone sharing the dream and teamwork of a ministry. They hold their thoughts, reflections, needs, and wants tightly inside of them, preferring to keep their inner person hidden even from their spouse. This causes pain in a relationship and can become the thing that slowly cools the initial sparks of love in a marriage, leaving both partners encased in their individual loneliness.

The tendency to keep things private can spill over into the way a pastor leads his congregation as well. He can Lone Ranger it for years, refusing to give away any control to others or neglecting to train and equip church members to do the work of ministry themselves. And in much the same way that an inability or a refusal to let a spouse get close affects the intimacy of a marriage, pastors can find themselves feeling isolated and weighed down by the load they are attempting to shoulder alone.

It doesn't have to be this way, in marriage or in ministry. When we grasp how desperately we need each other, we can see that God has made a provision not only for our loneliness but also for the growth and well-being of his church.

We Need Each Other

Just as there are many parts to our bodies, so it is with Christ's body. We are all parts of it, and it takes every one of us to make it complete, for we each have different work to do. So we belong to each other, and each needs all the others. (Rom. 12:4–5 TLB)

God uses the analogy of a body to describe the church because it's one we can understand; we can clearly see from looking at ourselves in a mirror that all the parts of our body need all the other parts for us to function well and be at optimum health.

First Corinthians 12:12–27 confirms this idea. The apostle Paul expands on the meaning behind the analogy when he writes in verse 21, "The eye cannot say to the hand, 'I don't need you!' And the head cannot say to the feet, 'I don't need you.'" Each part is necessary and important. The body has to have each part for it to work effectively. If my foot was chopped off, what would happen to my foot? It would die, and my leg would be incomplete. Not one body part can survive without the rest of the body for any length of time.

In your marriage, there's never a time your husband can legitimately tell you, "I don't need you." There's never a time you can legitimately tell your husband, "I don't need you." My friend, that goes against Scripture. God's Word says that you need him and he needs you. Any man who thinks he can pastor a church and not have his wife as a part of the team is a man who is sadly mistaken. He's a man who will find his ministry limited and even crippled because God intends for us to serve together—like a body in which each part is valued and needed.

I wonder if you realize *you* are your husband's most valuable resource for ministry—more than his education and training, more than his abilities, more than his spiritual gifts, more than anything. You are the most vital asset he has. I wonder if you realize *he* is your most valuable resource for ministry—more than your education and training, more than your abilities, more than your spiritual gifts, more than anything. He is the most vital asset you have. The truth is he needs you and you need him.

I'll tell you in more detail about my earlier view of myself in the next chapter, but in the beginning of our relationship, I was pretty sure Rick didn't need me. I saw him as incredibly talented and capable, and I saw myself as incredibly untalented and incapable. I kept trying to convince him he should find some other girl who was more biblically literate than I was, more talented, more gifted, and more self-assured. I was fairly certain I wasn't the right girl for him. It took a long time for him to convince me he needed me. Some of you might be in the same boat—you can identify. Even if you've been married for a long time, there could still be a gnawing fear in your heart that your husband really doesn't need you, that he really could do just fine without you. It's not true.

No individual is strong in every area. Good teams maximize strengths and minimize or compensate for weaknesses. Rick and I have applied this concept throughout our ministry, looking for ways our individual gifts and strengths complement and strengthen each other and the ministry. For example, Rick is an extrovert's extrovert, and he's very good with crowds. I don't understand how he does this, but he can walk into a room without knowing a soul and within seconds he's got them wound around his little finger. He tells stories, laughs at his own jokes, and gets people laughing, and before you know it, the whole room is turned toward him. He doesn't do it to manipulate. He's just being the outgoing person God made him to be. If you want a gathering to turn into a party, invite Rick!

At those same gatherings where he's enthralling the masses, I fare much better on a one-to-one level. I've always been an introvert, uncomfortable in a big-party atmosphere—you know, where the conversations stay at the fifty-thousand-foot level of superficiality and require bright smiles and snappy comebacks. Since the death of our son, my fondness for those environments has plummeted even farther; they require an energy expenditure that drains me completely. Give me the potted palm tree in the corner and a couple of people willing to engage and we'll spend the evening chatting on a soul level about the meaning of life, faith's mysteries, suffering, and world problems. The funny thing to me is that when Rick and I evaluate an event like that, he's happy if he's had the chance to shake hands and give hugs to all three hundred attendees, and I'm happy if I've had one or two soulful conversations. We are so different!

The strength of our differences is that not only can we share with each other a much fuller perspective on an event we attend, but God can also use our different personalities to reach people the other might not. You too can make your differences work to your advantage as a ministry-marriage team if you recognize each other's strengths and look for ways to leverage them for the benefit of your church. We are called to complement each other, not compare or compete.

For example, Rick is occasionally oblivious to the ways he unintentionally hurts people with his swift movements through a crowd. This is definitely a by-product of ADD as well as his extroverted temperament. I've always loved the way he goes out on the patio after a service and gives hundreds of hugs, takes a zillion photos with people, and makes himself available to our congregation and visitors. But there have been times I've watched an individual approach him to say something and he's only half listened, saying "Mm-hmm, mm-hmm, mm-hmm," and then pretty quickly disengaged to greet the next person or group waiting to take a photo. If I'm standing nearby, I can whisper in his ear, "Honey, that guy was trying to share something meaningful" or "That woman had a need and you didn't catch it." My sensitivity and ability to read people and then pass those insights on to him often allow him to go back and really engage in certain circumstances. And because of my strengths, he now takes a church counselor with him on the patio so he can hand over people who need extended care while he continues to interact with others waiting to speak to him. We are good for each other. He is more effective when I come along behind him, watching for reactions, and I am now better at standing on the patio engaging people in ways that don't come natural to me because he's taught me the power of the personal touch. Our ministry has become stronger and more effective as we've compensated for each other's weaker areas.

In smaller churches, there's no security team to protect you or intervene if someone gets out of control. It's up to you, and that's a lot of pressure. There's no backstage room where you can take a breath or get your bearings on a particularly stressful day. You're just out there and on. Negotiating the differences between extroverts and introverts and how much interaction with congregants and visitors is comfortable to you is a dance—like all of marriage—so listening to each other and valuing each other's strengths is key.

Here's another place where our differences work together for the good of the church. Rick is an amazing visionary with the spiritual gifts of faith and preaching. Visionaries see the big picture, and they see it in high definition. They do what I call "air painting," meaning they use their facial expressions, tone of voice, and usually big arm movements to "paint" a picture in the air that is so real most of us get caught up in the vision. They help us see with spiritual eyes something that might not even exist yet in the physical realm.

That's not me. Even though I refer to myself as a mystic, I have a very practical, down-to-earth side. I have the spiritual gifts of discernment and prophecy. So while Rick was busily "air painting" the launch of Saddleback Church for anyone who would listen, I was asking the practical questions: "Who is going to take care of the children who come to our new church? Who is bringing coffee and donuts? How will we transport the nursery equipment from our garage to the high school we're renting?" If you corner a visionary and ask them such mundane questions, they will stare at you with a blank expression—and eventually get frustrated with the person trying to discuss real-world matters. At least my visionary does. Child care? Coffee? Transportation? Those are "minor" details that will work themselves out later, according to visionaries. Every visionary needs a problem solver. My visionary has always needed people like me to come along occasionally and yank his feet from the clouds and plant them firmly on the ground. And he keeps me seeing the big picture behind all my efforts. That is how we learned to be a team—we truly need each other! I supply strengths he doesn't have, and he supplies strengths I don't have, and in that way, we compensate for each other's weaknesses. We lead in our own unique way. This is the body at work—both in marriage and in ministry.

Pastors' wives often ask if it's okay for them to be interested in areas of ministry that are different from those of their husbands, and the answer is of course! You don't have to work shoulder to shoulder on the same projects to be a team with your husband. You can work for a common goal while doing different things in ministry. When the Jews rebuilt the wall of Jerusalem under Nehemiah's direction, half of the group worked on rebuilding the wall and half of the group protected those who were building the wall. What would have happened if everybody had built the wall? There were enemies waiting to slaughter them. What if everybody had been out protecting? The wall would not have gotten built. It took the two teams working together to get the work of God done. They were working for a common goal, even though they were doing different things.

⟶ Sharing the Dream, Family Style ⟵

Let's be honest here—clergy kids have it tough in many ways. They face the same challenges we face, only they have to face them from an early age. They also have to do their maturing and growing under the scrutiny and attention of sometimes unkind church members or adults with unreasonable expectations.

That's why I devote a later chapter to raising children in a ministry home. For now, this section focuses on practical ways to help your children share the dream.

I really believe there is no greater heritage than for children to see that ministry is not just for dads but also for moms and brothers and sisters. At some point, your children have to catch the dream as well. If your children do not become a part of the dream that God has for you and your husband, they will become bitter and disillusioned and will resent every time the phone rings, every time you're away from them, every bit of time that is not poured out on them. On the other hand, if they catch the dream and understand that what you are doing is so much bigger than your family, it will reduce the resentment they might feel about the time you spend away from them. Here are three ways to help them catch the dream.

First, teach your children to pray for the ministry God has called you to. When my son Josh was six, we began negotiations for land to build our first building. The church was having trouble coming up with the financing, and it looked like the deal was not going to go through. It was an anxious time for us. Rick launched a church-wide prayer effort, and our kids joined in. Every night at bedtime Josh was faithful to pray. I confess that many times I would forget. I'd be in a hurry to end my day, thinking, *It's bedtime. The parenting clock says my shift is over.* He would call me back and say, "Mommy, we didn't pray for the land." Then he would pray sweet prayers like, "Dear God, I know you're going to give us that land. I know you're going to convince that banker to give us the money we need." Amy and Josh (at eight and six) had so much faith, and their faith really kept me going during the times when I felt discouraged about acquiring land and buildings for Saddleback.

Another way to help your children catch the dream is to teach them from an early age to cheerfully and regularly give financially to the Lord. This makes them feel they are a part of the things that matter to you and gives them a sense of ownership in your family's investment in a particular place. When our kids were very small—toddlers, really—we gave them an allowance of thirty cents: a dime for church, a dime for spending, and a dime for saving. You say, "That wasn't very even. You had them tithing more than 33 percent!" Hey, it made it easy for me! Ten cents went in this box, ten cents went in this box, and ten cents went in this box. They didn't know they were over-tithing. They were just excited to be giving.

Through the various land and building campaigns, they gave from their own resources. Sometimes they sold toys, cherished baseball cards, and other items that were special to them so they could participate in giving sacrificially. This was always their decision, not ours, but we provided a model of sacrificial giving they could adopt. Again, the point was to teach God's ownership of everything we hold dear—our time, our money, and our talents—and to provide them opportunities to share in the life of our church and God's kingdom.

A third way you can involve children is to give them a job in the ministry. You don't have to wait until they're teenagers to do this. Our daughter, Amy, was a child care worker on Sunday mornings by the time she was nine and continued on well into high school. We had three services on Sunday at the time, so she attended her own Sunday school class during the first service, sat with me during the second service, and worked in the preschool Sunday school classes during the third service. It was her ministry, and she loved it. She felt valued by the ways she contributed to our church. As she grew, her passion for hurting people led her to ministering to the homeless in Los Angeles and an outreach to people living with AIDS.

When Josh was ten, he became an usher. His station was by one set of stairs in the worship center, and he stood there cheerfully handing out bulletins, giving a warm welcome to all. He took it so seriously; if an adult came and tried to take that position from him, it really hurt his feelings. Josh also helped at the tape ministry table (before MP3s!), sold donuts, served as a helper with babies and toddlers, served as a Sunday school teacher for elementary-aged kids, and was a small group leader for high school boys when he was in college.

Even though Matthew had lifelong challenges, he served in the recycling ministry, digging through trash to collect bottles and cans that were turned into money to buy Bibles given away on mission trips; worked in child care; and was a small group leader for elementary-aged boys when he was in his teens. All our kids attended the annual trip to Mexico during spring break, serving Jesus with brothers and sisters in another culture.

Some of you who are raising PKs could tell amazing stories of the ways your kids serve Jesus: running sound systems, playing in bands, leading worship, teaching Sunday school, cleaning the church building, picking up trash, handing out bulletins, doing yard work at church, painting buildings, holding garage sales to raise money for mission projects, and so on. Hopefully, those acts of service create a sense of belonging and ownership more than they create resentment or the feeling of being used. If they are forced to do any of those things by either you as parents or the powers that be in the church, it's likely they will have a negative impact on your kids and their spiritual development. I would caution you to tread lightly and kindly here. Unfortunately, kids are pretty skilled at getting things mixed up in their minds—confusing who God is with the sometimes mean actions of church members or too-anxious-to-please-the-elders ministry parents.

I really believe the reason Amy and Josh care so deeply about the health and well-being of Saddleback Church today is because they have invested their prayers, their money, and their service since they were children. They understand what we're doing and why. They understand that the kingdom of God is so much bigger than our little family. They care passionately about the direction, the vision, the health, and the well-being of our staff as well as our members. Sometimes family conversations are intense as we, along with our son-in-love, daughter-in-love, and young grandchildren, emotionally and loudly discuss all things Saddleback Church. It makes for some wild and wooly discussions at times, but they come from a place of abiding love and decades of personal investment into the family of God we've been privileged to serve.

—— "I Believe in You" ——

Discussing how to share the dream leads me to ask another question. How long has it been since you told your husband, "I believe in you. I am 100 percent behind you and what you're doing. I don't understand it all, I'm even pretty scared about some of the plans, but I believe in you"? Maybe you've never put that thought into words before.

A few years ago after I shared this idea at one of our conferences, a pastor's wife approached me and said, "You know, I didn't realize I'd never said those words of affirmation to my husband. I guess I just assumed he knew I believed in him. I mean, why else would I stay with him through all the stuff we've been through? I could be off doing who knows what!" She went on to say, "I went home last night and told him, 'I believe in you, and I am 100 percent behind you in our ministry.' Through his tears he responded, 'I can't believe you care that much.'"

How long has it been since you told your husband you believe in him? How much you support him? No, he's not perfect, and he probably makes messes and mistakes occasionally. Maybe he says things that embarrass you or does things differently than you would do them. But he still needs to hear, "I admire you. I believe in you. I am so grateful to be the woman who gets to do life and ministry with you." It's just possible that if you share that with him and you mean it, he will have the courage to try things he would never have tried without your affirmation.

It comes down to this: we can be either dream builders or dream busters. Too many times I have been a dream buster. In my quest for practicality and my quest to yank Rick's feet back down to earth, I have been a dream buster rather than a dream builder or even a dream sharer. The simplest way to crush your husband, to quench the Spirit in his life, to put a damper on all God wants to do in him, is to be a dream buster. Every time he comes up with an idea, you say, "Oh, that won't work. We've tried that before. Don't you remember when you tried that and it was a total disaster? Don't you remember when so-and-so tried that and what happened with them?"

If, instead, you want to be a life giver to him, share his dream. That day so many years ago when I looked Rick in the eye and said, "I'm scared to plant a church, but I believe in God and I believe in you; let's do it!" changed the trajectory of our lives. My declaration of trust, faith, and belief in him melted his heart toward me. He still gets teary when he tells the story. Who knew those simple words spoken by a young, immature wife would resonate down the halls of our marriage for decades to come?

As you share in the ministry dream, you will begin to understand your importance and that you are vital to the success of God's ministry. And the shared dream for ministry will revitalize your marriage. As you work together as a team—sharing common goals and deep communication—you will grow in oneness and intimacy.

The Power of a Team over the Long Haul

A few of you might be thinking I'm making too big of a deal about sharing a dream and being a part of a team with your husband. You're not really convinced it's necessary. Your inclination is to brush aside the importance of seeking ways to join your worlds together, to focus less on your life as a couple and more on your life as a person. You might say, "I'm a woman before I'm a wife." So true! You and I *are* individual women before we are wives, mothers, daughters, sisters, friends, or ministers—and we will stand before God accountable first for our own lives and our own relationships with Jesus Christ. But at some point God may ask us, "How connected were you with that man in ministry? Were you one flesh only physically? Did you only share the same bed and have children together, or were you also one flesh with him emotionally? Were you one flesh with him spiritually?"

There are a thousand obstacles to oneness in marriage: dysfunctional families of origin, selfishness, immaturity, emotional wounds, broken trust, mental illness, addiction, an overcrowded lifestyle, season of life, differing views of what oneness even means—I suppose the list is never ending. To top it off, you can't make someone else be one with you; the other person has to choose it deliberately and freely day in and day out over the course of a lifetime. Maybe as you've read you've realized some repair work needs to happen in your marriage. Don't wait and don't put it off. Here's the motivation for doing the hard work of being one flesh:

> There is no limit to what God can do
> through a man and a woman
> walking side by side,
> hand in hand,
> sharing a dream.

Accepting Who You Are

The soul that has learned the blessed secret
of seeing God's hand in all that concerns it,
cannot be a prey to fear, it looks beyond all
second causes, straight into the heart and will
of God, and rests content, because He rules.

SUSANNAH SPURGEON,
wife of Charles Spurgeon

Y ou won't be in ministry for more than five minutes before you realize you've said yes to God in a way that will challenge every part of you; you've chosen one of the most difficult professions there is. It has unbelievable privileges, opportunities, and joys, but it also has unique pitfalls, discouragements, disappointments, and stresses. It's not an easy commitment or for anyone looking for a cushy life. Can I get a witness?

I want to be successful in ministry, and I want you to be successful too, but let me define the term. Rick and I have always taught that success in ministry is not about numerical results or recognition but about thriving, flourishing, and growing strong in one's calling and in one's character. I don't want to wearily collapse into retirement or leave ministry early because I'm burned out, bitter, disillusioned, cynical, or full of regret. Success is about living with integrity, passion, and a commitment to becoming like Christ; loving his church, his Word, his world, and the people he's made; personal growth in every area of life; gift development; and most of all finishing well.

To finish well, we must first start well and then live well, continually growing more skilled at navigating the twists and turns on the road of ministry. We have to be able to face the toughest circumstances with grace; build vibrant marriages and families in the glare of the spotlight; balance the competing needs of our churches, our families, and ourselves; maintain integrity at all times; point people to Jesus; speak up for those who cannot speak for themselves; and often do it all on a salary designed for college interns.

Clearly, this calls for us to be women of confidence, strength, and poise. How else can we possibly live well and finish well? And yet here's the problem. As I've talked to thousands of pastors' wives from every state and even around the world during the past forty years, I've heard one theme repeated by these dear sisters. Many live with a deep sense of inadequacy—a crippling lack of self-worth and self-confidence and a dreadful fear that they cannot possibly measure up to the expectations (real or perceived) that come with being a pastor's wife.

I've also met pastors' wives who ooze confidence, capability, and competence. They lead with great strength and self-assurance, and their challenges in ministry lie in a different direction. But more often than not, the women I talk to struggle with the way they view themselves. So for those of you who can't relate, be patient with the rest of us as we focus on developing a more accurate, realistic, and biblically based perception of ourselves. I believe every one of us is:

- ordinary
- capable
- secure

Ordinary Is Okay

I knew from an early age I was an ordinary person, and I was *not* happy about it. It felt like the kiss of death to me to be an average person. I yearned to shine in some special way, to be above average—to be *extra*-ordinary. As a child, I did my best to excel in academics; I worked diligently. Sad to say, as hard as I tried, I never earned straight As a single semester from kindergarten to college graduation. I did okay, but I was just an average student. That was discouraging to me, but it wasn't devastating. I told myself there were other avenues in which to excel and make my mark.

I wanted to learn how to play the piano, so my parents sacrificially scrimped and saved and bought an old refurbished player piano for the astronomical sum of $150. I took piano lessons and began to envision myself as a concert pianist who would travel the world and wow people with the beauty and passion of my music. Can you guess where this is going? I became a church pianist when I was twelve, but I discovered pretty quickly that I'm only average. The world tour as a concert pianist wasn't going to happen. Disappointment began to gather in my soul as now another way to make my mark proved unobtainable.

As I moved into my teenage years, I was still looking for the perfect way to distinguish myself and be more than average or ordinary. I "decided" I wanted to be beautiful—as though that's a decision any of us get to make—and set my sights on looking like Miss America. It didn't take me long to realize with deep sadness that I was never going to be a beautiful woman; I was going to be an average woman. Don't get me wrong. I know I'm not ugly—no one has ever fainted at the sight of me—but I wanted *more. I wanted to be beautiful.*

It seemed as though I struck out at everything I tried. My aspirations of academic excellence, musical excellence, and astounding beauty did not come to fruition. The things in life that I had thought would make me special and anything but average were out of my reach. I was just an ordinary girl.

Then I married Rick. Everything he touched turned to gold. Rick was good . . . at everything. In junior high and high school, he was student body president, excelled at academics, and was very popular. His mother proudly displayed his trophies in their living room. Far from ordinary.

When we started Saddleback, I was shy and lacked confidence in myself and my abilities. I felt Rick was already a superstar and had made a mistake by marrying me, a very ordinary woman. I taught children's Sunday school not because I was good with kids but because it was a safe place to hide out—they didn't know if I got the Bible story backward or not!

I'll never forget the moment when this issue of low self-worth and comparison came to a head. At twenty-six, I was an "older Christian woman" to the women who became believers and joined Saddleback in the early days, even though many of them were chronologically older than I was. They saw me as a mature believer, and I was given the responsibility of shepherding these new believers whether I felt capable of it or not.

The church organized a women's tea, and I was to be the speaker. As I drove to the event, I hit the wall emotionally and spiritually. I was completely overwhelmed by a deep sense of failure, inadequacy, and incompetence. I began to cry—hard— as my mind filled with scenes of my attempts to be the "best" pastor's wife ever. I got angry at God and hurled complaints at him as fast as I could think them up. "Why didn't you make me smarter? Why didn't you make me prettier? Why didn't you give me more talent and skills? Why didn't you give Rick a wife who was more suited to him? Why did you create me so average . . . so ordinary . . . so nothing?"

I realized I couldn't show up to this event with a tear-stained face, so I tried to distract myself. I turned on the local Christian radio station and heard an old song, "Ordinary People." The lyrics were an arrow of hope straight to my heart. "God chooses ordinary people. He chooses people just like you and me who are willing to give him their all—no matter how small their all might seem to them."

I have to tell you that moment completely changed my life. God parted the waters of my understanding. I finally got it that God had *intentionally* allowed me to be an average person; I didn't just stumble into being ordinary. He could have made me different—smarter, prettier, more talented—but he had *chosen me* to be an average, ordinary person. And that was okay! If God used only superstars, not much would get done, because he's made far more average, ordinary people than superstars.

My tears of complaint and frustration turned to tears of gratitude. I began to reflect on John 6, the passage this song is drawn from, and thought of the little boy and his small lunch offered to Jesus. A miracle took place from that lunch of loaves and fishes. Jesus multiplied the tiny offering into enough food for thousands of hungry people who were fed and satisfied.

All I had to offer to God was a tiny little lunch. In fact, I felt as if I had a tuna on white bread sandwich to offer to God while other people had salmon on brioche to give. My ordinariness felt like *nothing* in comparison.

But in that moment of clarity, God offered me the chance to adjust my self-perception and bring it more in line with the way he sees me. That day I had the chance to say, "God, I choose to believe you allowed me to be an average, ordinary person, and I thank you for making me this way. I want to be like the little boy in the Bible story who didn't have much to give to you but willingly gave it all. He didn't have a clue as to how Jesus was going to feed thousands of people from his small lunch, but he trusted that Jesus could do miracles. I don't know how you can do much with the little that I am, but all that I am and possess is yours. Will you multiply my offering and do a miracle? Will you do that in me?"

In the decades since that momentous day, I've been a witness to God's miracles as he has used the little I gave to him. He has opened doors of opportunity that still leave me speechless with amazement and gratitude. It doesn't make sense to me really—there's no human reason, no human achievements I can point to that would qualify me for some of the things I've gotten to be a part of. I wrote a book about this called *Say Yes to God*. At the end of the day, God is doing what he does best: transforming little into much.

You can make the same choice to adjust your perception of yourself. Are you going to continue to see yourself through the eyes of your childhood? Are you going to believe the lies that Satan and others have told you, about your abilities, about your capabilities, about who you are, and about who God has made you to be? Are you going to listen to them? Or are you going to adjust your perception of yourself and see yourself the way God does?

God may have made you an average and ordinary person. After all, he has made more average and ordinary people than superstars. The Bible is replete with stories of shepherds, no-mads, fishermen, and peasants with just a few kings, judges, wealthy landowners, and successful business owners thrown in. So it would not be unusual for you to say, "I am just an average person. I don't have any stellar, outstanding qualities that make me different from or head and shoulders above other people." But in ministry, this view can become a trap. It can become a place where the enemy discourages us and holds us down and makes us feel as if we have nothing significant to contribute.

This may be the most important prayer you pray after your salvation: "God, what I have to offer you doesn't seem very significant; it's certainly not awe-inspiring. There are so many other people more talented, more beautiful, more intelligent, and more gifted, people who know more than I do and can handle more than I can. But, God, this is what you've given me, and I give it back to you. I believe that little becomes much when

> Revel in the knowledge that God has *chosen* you to be who you are and that he loves you *exactly* the way you are!

it's placed in your hands, so I'm asking you to miraculously multiply my little."

If you want to keep the ministry from draining you dry, you must learn the strategies that help you cope with the difficulties, stresses, and pressures of the ministry. The first step is to accept the truth about who you are. Revel in the knowledge that God has chosen you to be who you are and that he loves you exactly the way you are. Believe he wants you to give him what you think is so small so that he can make something miraculous out of your life.

You Are More Capable Than You Think

Once we begin to see that most of us are ordinary people—not superstars—and are comfortable with that, the next challenge is to see ourselves as capable people.

Probably because I had a hard time accepting myself as an ordinary person, I didn't believe I had the capacity to make a contribution that God could really use and bless. Then I read a Scripture passage that rocked my inner world. Philippians 4:13 says, "I have strength for all things in Christ Who empowers me [I am ready for anything and equal to anything through Him Who infuses inner strength into me; I am self-sufficient in Christ's sufficiency]" (AMP-CE).

This has become an anchoring verse for my life. I want it on my tombstone! I think it's a verse that will anchor you too because it addresses the inner critic who relentlessly hurls accusations, passes judgments on us, and undercuts our confidence that we can serve and lead and minister effectively. If you're not sure you're familiar with this inner critic, hers is the voice you hear when you're putting on your makeup or brushing your teeth—those moments when you're staring at yourself in the mirror. This voice says things like, "You know, if people really knew you, they would see what a phony you are." Or "Look at _____; she can run circles around you. What makes you think you have what it takes to tackle that project or run that ministry? Girl, you were standing behind the door when they were handing out gifts. Give it up."

This inner voice can also lead us to argue with God about his calling for us. We end up playing a spiritual *Let's Make a Deal* with him. We say, "I'll take what's behind door number 1 but not door number 2" or "God, I'll serve you in *this* ministry but never in *that* one." Maybe you've said, "I'll set up chairs for the fellowship event after church, but I'm not leading a Bible study." Or "I'll do anything you want me to do here locally, God, but there's no way I'm traveling overseas on a mission trip."

I think you've experienced this at least once, where you set limits and parameters around your service to God as if he isn't the one who made you and knows how he's gifted you. When we set limitations on our obedience to God because of our fears or insecurities, we end up limiting our intimacy with him. We put distance between us and God when we tell him what we think we can do or what we're willing to do.

The truth is whatever God has called you to do, he will equip you to do! As Martha Davidson, a fellow pastor's wife, says, "Don't limit yourself by your fears or your gifts!"

God makes us capable in a remarkable way. As Philippians 4:13 says, "I am self-sufficient in Christ's sufficiency" (AMP-CE).

In other words, God has infused his strength into me. I'm not strong enough on my own, but through the strength Jesus provides—his personal resurrection power and strength—I can handle whatever God has asked me to do and be.

If you have not come to grips with the truth that you are self-sufficient in Christ's sufficiency, you will struggle throughout your ministry doubting whether you're really capable of the things God has asked you to do. This will limit your faith, which will in turn affect the churches or ministries you lead.

You Are Secure in Christ

Again, I'm not exactly sure why I was so fearful and anxious when I was growing up and early in my marriage—I've learned a lot about a long line of anxiety and depression in my family—but I frequently panicked that something might happen to Rick. Those fears were brought to a head one day at a pastors' conference Rick and I attended. The husbands and wives were separated into different tracks for part of the day, and the speaker in my session was a former pastor's wife. She told us she and her husband had served for many years as a ministry team. He had been the pastor of a large church and had had an important role in the community. But then her husband had become ill and died. She said, "When my husband was alive, our mailbox was full of speaking invitations from big conferences and other churches. Everybody wanted him to do this and be a part of that. Our lives were hectic and full. Then he died. The phone stopped ringing. Our mailbox was empty, and there were no more invitations to speak. I started to feel like I didn't belong anymore, not even in my own church." She vulnerably expressed her fears: "Maybe I only mattered because I was his wife."

When she said those words, a sharp knife went into my heart. I couldn't breathe.

In a daze, I stumbled back to our hotel room, where Rick was eagerly waiting to share all the great things that had happened in the session he had attended. He was also anticipating a nice evening alone together in a hotel room with no kids barging in—a rare treat for parents of elementary-aged children. He had no idea how shaken I was by the question vaguely forming in my head; he couldn't see the darkness that had descended on my soul or the fear that was holding my heart in a vise. Our conversation went like this:

Him: "How was your session?"

Me: "Terrible!"

Him: "Terrible? Why? What happened?"

Me: "Nothing."

Him: "Then what's wrong?"

Me: "I don't know! I'm just so depressed!"

Him: "But why?"

Me: "I don't know!"

Him: (bewilderment spreading on his face) "I don't understand why you're so upset."

Me: "Please, just leave me alone!"

Him: (suddenly aware that his plans for the evening were quickly disappearing into the hotel toilet) "Um . . . so I guess you don't want to make love, right?"

Me: "No!" (tears)

Completely beaten by my baffling responses, he went to sleep. I lay in the hotel bed staring at the ceiling, trying to get my heartbeat to slow down. Suddenly, it was crystal clear to me. My panicked response to the speaker's story was all about my carefully guarded fear that I mattered only because I was married to Rick Warren. Saddleback Church was thriving and demanded much of his attention. He was beginning to gain some acclaim; people were beginning to hear his name and know who he was. Our mailbox was full; he received more invitations than he could possibly accept. What if he were to leave me or die? What if he became ill and was incapacitated and was unable to pastor any longer? Would I still matter? Would there be a place for me? Would I have any significance apart from this man I had spent so much of my life with?

I cried out through my tears, "God, you've got to help me because I've got stuff really mixed up in my head. I can't serve you with my whole heart if I have to live in fear every day that I'm not going to matter if something happens to Rick—that I'm not important without Rick."

That middle-of-the-night divine conversation was life changing. God very gently reminded me of a passage of Scripture I had just taught on the week before. Forgive me if I adapt the passage a tiny bit, but this is how the Holy Spirit applied these verses to my life.

> Cursed is the woman who trusts in man,
> who draws strength from mere flesh
> and whose heart turns away from the LORD.
> She will be like a bush in the wastelands;
> she will not see prosperity when it comes.

> She will dwell in the parched places of the desert,
> in a salt land where no one lives.
> But blessed is the woman who trusts in the LORD,
> whose confidence is in him.
> She will be like a tree planted by the water
> that sends out its roots by the stream.
> She does not fear when heat comes;
> her leaves are always green.
> She has no worries in a year of drought
> and never fails to bear fruit. (Jer. 17:5–8)

What comfort and assurance to know that I don't matter because I'm married to Rick Warren. I don't matter because I'm a pastor's wife of Saddleback Church. I matter because God thought me up. He saved me and preserves me, and he's waiting eagerly for the day when we will see each other face-to-face. I matter because I am his beloved daughter.

God says this is what I should be grateful for:

> But we should always give thanks to God for you, brethren beloved by the Lord, because God has chosen you from the beginning for salvation through sanctification by the Spirit and faith in the truth. (2 Thess. 2:13 NASB)

Not only am I "beloved by the Lord," but I've been chosen by God:

> So, as those who have been chosen of God, holy and beloved, put on a heart of compassion, kindness, humility, gentleness and patience. (Col. 3:12 NASB)

The cold, hard reality is Rick could leave me. I don't believe for one second that's ever going to happen, and I never worry about it now, but sometimes people do things we never expect. He could have a stroke and become incapacitated, never able to preach another sermon; our lives could change in an instant. Rick could die before I do. For sure, someday, we'll leave Saddleback Church so the next generation can lead it. At that point, I will no longer be able to hold on to my role and status as the senior pastor's wife. But I am a secure woman. My confidence and security are in God, not in the man I married or the church we pastor. The strong Word of God tells me my value, my worth, and my importance can never be affected in the slightest by any changes that come my way.

Unless you settle this issue for yourself, you will constantly be anxious, unsure of where your value comes from, questioning whether you are important in God's kingdom apart from your husband and your church. You are a valuable woman simply because God Almighty loves you, created you, died for you, and will come to take you home with him someday. He has good plans for you—plans to use you and your gifts. Don't let anxiety about why you matter sidetrack you.

> My *confidence* and security are in *God*, not in the man I married or the church we pastor.

By the way, women aren't the only ones who get caught in this trap of evaluating their worth by external standards. These are broad generalizations, but if some women find their value in their relationships, some men find their value in their work. The good news, though, is that the same wonderful truth applies to both. Your husband doesn't have worth and value by virtue of the church he serves or the role he plays. Your husband doesn't have value because of what other pastors say about him. Your husband doesn't have worth because of the size of the ministry he has built. Even if he doesn't experience the success he was hoping for, or loses his job, or has a health problem and is incapacitated, or has to leave the ministry due to a failure, he still matters to God. He is still a beloved son of God. Nothing can diminish his status in God's eyes.

You cannot thrive in ministry if you waste your emotional energy wishing God had made you differently. You cannot thrive in ministry if you cower in fear before the tasks and goals he has laid out before you. You cannot thrive in ministry if you think you're valuable because of an external measurement—your husband's job or the particular church you serve. You matter because you are God's beloved.

⟞ The Truth That Frees You ⟝

When we relax and embrace who we are, an incredible inner liberty is unleashed deep in our souls. We're able to move freely in life and ministry, confident that God will multiply our ordinariness into miracles, confident we are "self-sufficient in Christ's sufficiency," confident we are capable and competent for any task he asks us to do, and confident that our value as a person is secure and settled because we are God's beloved, regardless of all that happens in our lives.

So do I still struggle in these areas? Yep, every so often I do. Sometimes authors and speakers make it sound as though all of their struggles are in the past; *now* they are completely whole and healed and no longer fail or mess up. Don't believe them. They're lying to themselves and to you. Hebrews 10:14 says, "For by one sacrifice he has made perfect forever those who are being made holy." According to this verse, sanctification—the process of becoming like Christ in our character—is both a once-and-for-all moment in time ("made perfect forever") and a moment-by-moment sweaty wrestling match between who we were and who we are becoming ("those who are being made holy").

This means we don't always get it right. Sometimes there's a gap. But what's reassuring is that God will never stop working on our character until Christ is formed in us; this process of being made holy will last until Jesus comes for us. We can be patient with ourselves and each other. As Paul says, "And I am sure that God who began the good work within you will keep right on helping you grow in his grace until his task within you is finally finished on that day when Jesus Christ returns" (Phil. 1:6 TLB).

When I was writing the first chapter of this book, I had a day of complete self-doubt—I mean, I was a puddle on the floor. I was hit with a tsunami wave of no self-confidence, severe dislike of my ordinariness, and acute cravings to be somebody else—someone more beautiful, more spiritually mature, and definitely more talented. I had a long list in my head of all the women I wanted to be instead of me that afternoon. I was feeling so despondent that I sent out a message on Instagram that practically begged for reassurance that I was okay, that I was good enough, that I was loved, and that a few people would read my book. After I hit the "share" button, I was filled with remorse. "Kay Warren," I said angrily, "how pathetic is it to cast a plea into cyberspace to people you don't even know and expect them to soothe your messed-up psyche?"

Wonderful people kindly responded back with "atta girl" and "we love you" and "we'll read your book," and the messages propped up my sagging self-confidence for a little while. But I bypassed the one true source of self-confidence—God's Word and the truth it reveals about whose I am and who God has made me to be. I blew it. So, yeah, I still forget sometimes that God has made me ordinary for a reason (so I will depend on him), fills me with Christ's sufficiency for any and all things, and loves me whether I write a book or never do anything again besides lie on the couch popping crunchy Cheetos.

You too can be confident he won't stop his good work in you until the day you die. He won't stop reminding you that he specializes in multiplying little into much. He'll continue to pour his sufficiency into you, giving you the strength, energy, and passion you need to fulfill his calling. He will whisper to you every day that you matter because he chose you, he loves you, and you belong to him. You, my sister, are ready for anything and equal to anything through the resurrection power of Jesus Christ.

4

Adapting to Change

I know not what He is about to do with me, but
I have given myself entirely into His hands.

CATHERINE BOOTH,
wife of William Booth

———

We live on a corner lot on the edge of a small canyon in Southern California. The famous Santa Ana winds—measured by our neighbor's wind meter at more than 90 mph—can come up at any hour of the day between December and February. That means we can go to bed at 10 p.m. with the air still and serene only to be awakened in the middle of the night by howling winds that uproot trees, fling patio furniture into the pool, and strip foliage off plants down to the bare stalks. Believe it or not, we weren't warned about the wind in the canyon before we moved into our new home in early December of 1992. We wearily dropped into bed the first night after a heavy day of moving, expecting blissful sleep. Within a few hours, the five of us were suddenly yanked from our slumber by a violent wind that shook the doors and windows and terrified us all. I confess my first dazed and confused thought was that we were either in the middle of the rapture or under nuclear attack—the noise and movement of the house were overwhelming. At the very least, I thought the wind was going to dislodge our house and set it down in Kansas like in *The Wizard of Oz!*

Isn't that a metaphor for life? We know things don't stay the same, but when the winds of change blow through and topple our routine, we're still shocked. I'm not a very flexible person. I don't particularly like change—especially rapid or chaotic change, change that I wasn't anticipating. Let's be honest—I like control. Control is good! I prefer all my little ducks in a row with everything and every person neat and organized. I discovered the real-life basis for this phrase this spring when a mama duck hatched her eleven ducklings in our backyard and tried to make our pool their new home. Rick videotaped himself gently shooing them out of our yard. I laughed to see what the ducklings did when they were alarmed. In a flash, their God-given instincts kicked in and they scrambled to align themselves with military precision into two neat rows behind their mama. But people and circumstances are not like ducklings that automatically fall into neat, manageable rows. God has had his work cut out for him teaching me how to gracefully adapt to the changes that have come.

A life in ministry is similar. Nothing remains the same from day to day: the people in your congregation change, their needs change, the community around you changes, the culture changes, your family changes, you change. Not all change is bad, however, and the trick is to distinguish between good, healthy change and what must *not* change regardless of how wildly the ground shifts beneath your feet or how fiercely the winds blow around you.

In our years at Saddleback, we've changed the structure, the location, the buildings, and the programs; we've changed our approach, our music style, and our personnel. Our hair has changed, our weight has changed, our health has changed, our income has changed, and our family has changed. Very little about our lives is the way it was when we began in 1980.

In the very early years of the church, Rick and I each wore a lot of hats. He was the visionary, strategist, and lead pastor. He preached the weekend services, did any midweek teaching, did all the baptizing, and performed all the weddings and funerals. I did just about everything else. Initially, I was the church pianist, church secretary, nursery and preschool coordinator, and Sunday school teacher. One of the great things as the church has grown has been the opportunity to take off some of those hats that didn't particularly fit my personality or my spiritual gifts and begin to specialize in ministries more suited to who I am. I was the first volunteer women's ministry director and lead women's Bible study teacher. I taught CLASS 101, our church membership class, for years. Eventually, I was able to specialize in areas that were even more of a passion as I served in the college ministry and then became the first HIV & AIDS Initiative director at Saddleback. Now I'm the catalyst behind the expansion of Saddleback's mental health ministry. So many different roles and hats I have worn over these years! Each one of those changes also required an ability to adapt.

One of the surprises I didn't anticipate was that I would experience sadness and even grief as the church grew. Typically, we expect that numerical growth is a positive change, and it is in many ways if it means more people are coming to know Jesus as their Savior or accessing the help and services the church provides in the community. I just didn't realize it also would be painful to me.

Since we started Saddleback with seven people, hospitality was an integral part of church planting. Every meeting and Bible study was held in our home, and I enjoyed it. I enjoyed preparing a meal with the couples and singles who kept joining our little band of pioneers. We would eat and talk and pray and dream. Then in the first year of the church, I invited everyone who joined the church to have dinner in our home at least once. That meant I prepared the same meal two nights a week and invited two families to join us. Then following in the footsteps of Rick's mom, who was the most hospitable woman I've ever met, I decided to host an open house at Christmas for the congregation, which I did for the next five years. I did all the baking from scratch—I corralled the wives of our first paid staff members into baking like mad women with me—and I loved it. I also hosted the Church Chat in our home every month to welcome newcomers. But then the church grew really fast, and we weren't able to hold events in our house because it was too small and the numbers were too large. I had to stop having the Christmas open house the year after we ran five hundred people through our fourteen-hundred-square-foot house and yard in one afternoon. I cried when I realized I couldn't offer hospitality anymore in the way that meant something to me. I had to give up something I dearly loved when the size of the church made it impossible to keep it going.

Today people walk up to me on the patio and say, "I've been a church member for ten years, and I've always wanted to meet you." I cry on the inside when I hear those words because I used to know every family, every single man and woman, their children, their aunt Sue, and their dog. There's a principle at work here—an often ignored or minimized principle: there's a price to pay for a growing church. It might not be the loss of having people in your home or giving up an activity you love, but somewhere you will experience the sadness of change. Go ahead and feel it. Shed a few tears if you want to. Then turn your thoughts to gratitude for people coming to know Jesus and know the result is worth the cost.

Three Questions to Guide You through Change

Have you ever felt as though everybody in the church has an agenda for your life—a set of expectations of what they think you *should* be doing at any given moment in time? Pastors' wives are commonly asked or expected to participate in or lead a particular area of ministry in the church, and deciding what *you* really want to be a part of can be a cause of anxiety and confusion. It's never fun to serve or lead out of guilt, duty, or pressure, and it's especially not pleasant to serve in an area that feels unsuited to who you are as a person. Pastors' wives—and not just those new to ministry—frequently ask, "How do I know what I'm supposed to be involved in? Are there guidelines I can follow?"

We've all had to deal with what Sister So-and-So (and sometimes our husband) has in mind for us, so I want to share with you the three clarifying questions I ask myself to help me evaluate ministry opportunities. A caveat, though, before I share the three questions. There are situations and seasons when you don't get to take off all those hats that don't really fit you; you may not have the opportunity to do the thing you love the most because of circumstances. I've been there, but it's still important to ask the following three questions so that you're able to move toward the ministries that bring you joy in service as circumstances allow.

What Is My SHAPE?

SHAPE is a way of teaching the five components of how God has contoured us uniquely based on Job 10:8: "Your hands shaped me and made me." Your SHAPE determines absolutely everything about you—the kind of person you are, your likes and dislikes, what drives you, and your outlook on life. Everything about you can be understood by your SHAPE. This acrostic that Rick developed makes it easy to remember the five components. SHAPE stands for:

> S—spiritual gifts
> H—heart
> A—abilities
> P—personality
> E—experiences

SPIRITUAL GIFTS

Many excellent books have been written about spiritual gifts, so I just want to remind you how important it is to consider your spiritual gifts when you take an inventory of the ways God has formed you as a unique person equipped to serve. Anytime you consider a ministry opportunity, start with your spiritual gifts.

In 1 Corinthians 12:4–11, the apostle Paul brilliantly explains spiritual gifts—gifts given to each believer by the Holy Spirit to be used for the common good. In verses 7 and 11, he says, "A spiritual gift is given to each of us so we can help each other. . . . It is the one and only Spirit who distributes all these gifts. He alone decides which gift each person should have" (NLT).

I believe my spiritual gifts are prophecy, teaching, and discernment, and my primary spiritual gift is teaching. I never would have known that about myself if I hadn't gotten over my fear of being an ordinary person and decided to take a risk and lead a Bible study for five women. I didn't know how to study the Bible for myself. I knew how to read it, and I knew how to fill in the answers to a curriculum, but I didn't know anything about studying and leading and teaching the Bible. But those five women responded to my feeble attempts to teach and lead using a fill-in-the-blank curriculum I had bought at the local Christian bookstore. To my astonishment, they grew in their newfound faith. They started to see answers to prayer. They developed more Christlike attitudes and behavior. They became more loving wives and moms. Their faith expanded. It blew me away!

I still wasn't very skilled at teaching, although I was excited to learn. I took a class on how to be a Christian public speaker and learned how to craft an effective message. I asked trusted friends to give me honest critique and feedback, and I learned from their suggestions. I started practicing every chance I got. I even began to offer myself to other ministries within the church as a speaker and took a few outside speaking engagements. At first, and for quite some time, I was terrified and often felt as if I slipped a "coat" on when I stood up to speak—I was confident and assured—but then slipped the "coat" off as I stepped away from the podium. For many years I had a difficult time reconciling the teacher part of me with the shy introvert who didn't like attention.

Slowly, over the years, I found that teaching wasn't a chore anymore or even hard work. I found that I love to teach more than almost anything else. I feel fully alive when I am teaching the Bible or calling people to biblical behavior and action, especially when I have the chance to speak on behalf of those who have little to no voice. The young woman who sobbed on her way to speak to a few women at a women's tea in 1982 is pretty much just a memory. In her place is a woman who is never more vibrantly alive than in the incredible moments of partnership with Almighty God, preaching and teaching the words I believe he has given.

God chooses the gifts for us and assures us that we have received at least one gift. Are you aware of your spiritual gifts? Are you using them to the best of your ability in your current life situation? Are you fearful of exploring the possibilities? It's okay to experiment and see if something fits. And most of all, be a wise steward of what you've been given and maximize it for God's glory and the health of his church. Get more training, more experience, and more development. Magnify the gifts you've been given through hard work, practice, discipline, and courage.

HEART

Proverbs 27:19 says, "It is your own face that you see reflected in the water and it is your own self that you see in your heart" (GNT).

"Heart" in the acrostic SHAPE refers to your passions, your drives, the things that get you up in the morning and make your heart beat faster with enthusiasm. Not only do you have a unique physical heartbeat, but you also have a unique emotional heartbeat. I'm not referring to your personality. I'm referring to the things that drive you and give you such pleasure and joy in serving God.

One of the passions that drives me and is so close to my heart is encouraging believers not to walk away from God, to fully trust him no matter what, to develop an intimacy with God that is so deep and true and real that no amount of suffering can destroy it. I am repetitive. I endlessly talk about it because it is a core passion of mine. My heart comes alive when I encourage believers not to give up or walk away from God when circumstances get tough.

I also have a passion for people living on the margins—those who have little to no voice in this world. People living with HIV, orphans and vulnerable children, people living with a mental illness and struggling with suicidal thoughts and actions—these are human beings who stir my heart deeply. I have a genuine desire for these three groups of people to be free from stigma and ill treatment and receive the support they need to survive and thrive. I am driven to speak up for them, to use my voice and my platform on their behalf. If I'm not talking about developing intimacy with God, I'm talking about mental illness, HIV, or orphans and how the church of Jesus Christ is called to be engaged in practical, sacrificial ways—and I especially love it when I can weave all these passions into one message!

If you're not sure how to identify the drivers of your heart, try to visualize yourself on a day with no responsibilities, no obligations—perhaps lying on the beach in the sun. What topics surface when your mind is still and quiet? What can't you stop thinking about? The themes or people who are always on your mind often offer a vital clue to the passions of your heart and the motivations that drive you.

This matters because when we're doing work we love, we are more productive than when we're spending our time and energy on work we dislike. Living by your heart is one of the keys to being effective. As Rick says, find what you love to do—what God has made you to do—and do it for his glory.

ABILITIES

Consider the following verses:

The women skilled in sewing and spinning prepared blue, purple, and scarlet thread and cloth, and fine-twined linen, and brought them in. Some other women gladly used their special skill to spin the goats' hair into cloth. (Exod. 35:25–26 TLB)

[The LORD] has filled them with skill to do all kinds of work as engravers, designers, embroiderers in blue, purple and scarlet yarn and fine linen, and weavers—all of them skilled workers and designers. (Exod. 35:35)

Then Moses summoned Bezalel and Oholiab and every skilled person to whom the LORD had given ability and who was willing to come and do the work. (Exod. 36:2)

Abilities are the natural talents we possess. These verses tell us that even our natural abilities are God-given; they are given to every person and differ from spiritual gifts, which only Christians possess. There may have been moments when you thought you didn't have *any* abilities, but scientists tell us we each have between five hundred and seven hundred abilities. We don't always think of being able to lift our arm above our head as an ability, but if you can't do it, believe me, you recognize the loss of that ability.

I have zero abilities in math, science, or business—I *stink* at all three subjects. I break into a cold sweat when my grandchildren ask for math homework help. I mean, I couldn't do it when I was in fourth grade. What makes me think I can do it now? It's not like it got any easier over the past few decades. Ask me to explain the laws of thermodynamics, and I'm toast. Quote from some current business guru and watch my eyes glaze over in seconds. I simply do not care.

But I thoroughly enjoy English vocabulary and grammar, history, and music. Ask me the etymology of any word, and I'll fall over myself to look it up. My thirteen-year-old granddaughter, Kaylie, and I try to outdo each other in finding the most obscure word to use in our conversations. We don't have to know what the word means, but we have to be able to spell it correctly. Talk to me about life in any period of history, and you've got my attention. Music is as necessary as air to me; it feeds my soul and is a constant companion.

You know what I love most? Details! My affectionate title at Saddleback, given to me by some of the staff, is Minister of Small Things. I love to look at plans or proposals and find the holes. Rick has said sometimes in frustration, "Why aren't you more positive? Why do you always see the negatives and find the holes in things? How about finding all the things that are wonderful in this plan?" Yeah, I see the wonderful things, but I also see where something is lacking or missing. It's just part of the way God has made me and the abilities he has given me. It makes me a terrific proofreader. In fact, for probably the first fifteen years at Saddleback, no weekly bulletin or major print piece went to press without me laying my eyes on it first.

How about you? What abilities come so naturally to you that you don't even have to think about them? In what areas do people compliment you and say, "You're so good at _____"? Frequently, we are dismissive of those compliments, thinking, *Well, everybody does that!* We tend to minimize our natural abilities because we are so comfortable doing them that they don't seem very significant; we don't realize they are truly abilities others don't have. What abilities has God given to you, and how do they play a part in helping you figure out where to serve in ministry?

PERSONALITY

How has God uniquely shaped you in this vital aspect of who you are? Are you more of an extrovert or an introvert? Are you somewhere in between? Are you a neat freak or a slob—or something in between? Do you feel things intensely, or are you more even-keeled? Do you enjoy activities that involve risk, or do you prefer the tried and true? Do you find rules something to be broken, or does following the rules seem the most logical course of action? Do you enjoy processing your thoughts with other people, or do you prefer to keep them to yourself until you come to a conclusion? We're all so different!

I'm pretty intense. I'm an introvert and a melancholy by some personality definitions; I feel *all* of my emotions deeply. I might give the impression that I'm an extrovert because I love to teach and appear comfortable on the stage or in the spotlight, but I am not an extrovert by temperament or personality. I have always had a degree of social anxiety, and as I've told you, my natural bent in a social setting is to find the potted palm tree in the room and stand there with one person for the next hour and share deeply about our lives. I don't naturally want to seek out each person in the room and say, "How do you do? It's nice to meet you." I can do it when I'm traveling and doing speaking engagements—audience members usually expect to greet speakers and engage with them a bit—but it's an acquired skill. I've learned to do it because it's an important part of God's calling on my life, but it will probably never be *easy* for me.

There's an insidious, unspoken assumption that only extroverts can *really* serve God; it's something that both introverts and extroverts believe. We get caught in the trap of elevating one personality type over the other—even to ourselves—and that breaks my heart. God has deliberately created us with a widely diverse array of personality characteristics, traits, and quirks, and each variation is a delight to him. Each is intended to reveal some aspect of who God is, and each is needed in the body. You easygoing, nothing-rattles-you people—thank you for spreading calm over our chaos. You highly organized, get-it-done-my-way people—nothing would ever be accomplished without you. You intense, highly sensitive, introspective feelers—you make us see life through a lens of compassion. You over-the-top, energetic balls of energy—thank you for making us laugh and play. How does your particular personality shape ministry for you?

EXPERIENCES

As we evaluate how God's hands have formed and shaped us for ministry, we must realize that the most significant element is our life experiences. All of them—the good, the bad, and the ugly. It's helpful to ask yourself some basic questions about your life experiences: "What kind of a home did I grow up in? What were my educational experiences? Who have been my closest friends? What have been my career experiences? What have been the best moments so far? What have been the most painful experiences?"

I already told you I grew up in the home of a conservative pastor. I was the only child until I was eight, and then my brother, Andy, was born. Our home was quiet and peaceful, with a lot of love and kindness. We moved several times during my younger years when my father changed pastorates. I was always the new kid, never quite feeling like I fit in. I was an average student. My entire social life revolved around the church and its activities. I knew very little outside of my church and my home. I went to a Christian college where I met Rick, and we eventually started Saddleback Church. I had three beautiful children. I get to write, teach, preach, and minister widely.

But as I've already told you, it hasn't all been positive or pleasant. As I mentioned in chapter 1, I was molested as a little girl by the adolescent son of our church janitor. I struggled with a pornography habit. Rick and I had severe marriage problems for many years. I've had breast cancer and melanoma. Our youngest son lived with mental illness and died by suicide.

I am who I am today because of my life experiences—lovely, joyous, fulfilling, satisfying, wounding, frightening, horrifying, devastating. All of them have combined to form and shape me. Of course, there are some experiences I would trade in a heartbeat. At the same time, I'm profoundly aware of the ways God has molded me for *his* purposes.

So reflect on your life experiences. What good things have happened to you? How did school/educational experiences shape you? What career choices have affected who you are today? What painful things have happened to you? What are the secrets from your past? How do they affect you now? And how do all of these pieces of who you are fit together? Your spiritual gifts, heart, abilities, personality, and experiences—how do they all come together to shape you to be an effective minister for God?

When you play a board game, there's often a space labeled "start." These questions and reflections about your SHAPE are the "start" button as you evaluate the service opportunities before you in ministry. They provide a concrete launching point for you to assess what areas of ministry truly fit the way God has made you. They reveal what you're likely to be good at and where you're likely to struggle in finding fulfillment and effectiveness.

Whose Voice Am I Listening To?

If asked whose advice we should pay attention to—whose voice we are supposed to listen to above any other voice—we would all dutifully say, "God's. I'm supposed to listen to God." But in reality, we frequently listen to everybody else's voice but God's. We listen to what our husband says. We listen to Mrs. So-and-So, wife of the chairman of the deacons or elder board, who really, really believes we are supposed to be doing XYZ. Or we listen to a friend we admire and respect. Sometimes the combined voices in our heads are a cacophony of sound that drowns out the whisper of God's Spirit. It's not that we shouldn't seek advice or counsel from those around us, but we make the mistake of talking to them *first*. As the psalmist reminds us, it's God's voice we need to hear first and foremost: "Let me hear of your unfailing love each morning, for I am trusting you. Show me where to walk, for I give myself to you" (Ps. 143:8 NLT).

God promises to give us wisdom when we ask in prayer.

> If you want to know what God wants you to do, ask him, and he will gladly tell you, for he is always ready to give a bountiful supply of wisdom to all who ask him; he will not resent it. But when you ask him, be sure that you really expect him to tell you, for a doubtful mind will be as unsettled as a wave of the sea that is driven and tossed by the wind. (James 1:5–6 TLB)

So if you are presented with an opportunity to serve and feel pressured to jump in but are uncertain whether it's right for you in this season of life or whether it fits your SHAPE, stop and ask yourself whose voice is calling to you. Is it a human voice? Or is it God's voice? If it's a human voice, avoid it like the plague. Don't do it. Our prime allegiance is to God, not another human being, no matter how "important" they may seem or how compelling their voice may be.

It's extremely difficult for some women to say no to their pastor/husband. After all, he's the one with the supposed direct line to God, right? Wrong. As wonderful or godly as he is, he doesn't automatically have a

> Our prime **allegiance** is to God, not another human being, no matter how "important" they may seem or how *compelling* their voice may be.

stronger connection to God than you do; you both contain the Spirit of God, and he will speak to you. Of course, God uses our husbands, children, friends, strangers, and even enemies to speak to us at times, but we can hear God's voice just as well as they can. When we honestly, sincerely seek God's face and are living in surrender to his will, we can be certain that he will speak to us and give us direction about where to serve him.

Then it might come down to being willing to disappoint one of the other voices. We'll talk about this further in chapter 10.

Is My Prayer Life Sufficient to Cover This New Responsibility?

Not only do we need to talk to God in prayer about what he wants us *to do* in ministry, but we also have to be willing to spend time praying *for* any ministry we might accept. We have to take an honest and realistic look at our current responsibilities and ponder the actual time we will have to pray for this potential new responsibility.

We are to live from the inside out, not from the outside in, to go through our days operating out of internal conviction and assurance, not out of external pressure and obligation. We're to live from our heart and soul, not from reactions to external circumstances and events. We're to live Spirit-driven lives, completely dependent on him, not self-driven lives, completely dependent on ourselves. If our prayer life is already overwhelmed by too many commitments and responsibilities—and we say yes anyway—we're doomed. Or rather, I should say, the new ministry opportunity is doomed.

As we begin to feel the weight of the new ministry we've committed to—knowing the whole time that we simply cannot give it the prayer time it deserves—we will struggle and work in our flesh rather than in the Spirit, be driven by pressure and obligation rather than by conviction and assurance, and live from the outside in rather than from the inside out.

Perhaps you can remember a time when you reluctantly said yes to a ministry responsibility as a favor to someone else—you bailed a friend out of a jam because she was too swamped to do it. Consider this. If you say yes out of a sense of duty or guilt to a ministry you can't honor with prayer, not only will you be overextending yourself, but you also could be robbing someone else of the joy of participating in that ministry. Trust that God cares more about the proposed ministry than you do, and it's up to him to provide the volunteers. Sometimes that means a ministry will slow down or cease for a period of time because there is no one to staff it. Remind yourself that it's better for you to live from the inside out, depending on God in prayer, than to take on more than you already know is too much for you. Do yourself and the ministry a favor: say no. Say not now. Say maybe later or in another season. But don't keep piling responsibility on top of responsibility when you know you cannot pray for the ministry and the precious people it reaches. Sometimes no is a very godly answer.

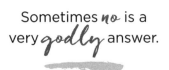

Sometimes *no* is a very *godly* answer.

The next time somebody says, "You really need to be involved in this ministry/project/event. You are the right person to do this!" stop and ask these three clarifying questions: Does it use my SHAPE? Whose voice am I listening to? Can my prayer life cover it?

▬ Trusting the Change God Brings ▬

I can't move on from this conversation without also saying that sometimes God blows up all of our carefully crafted formulas and lists and asks us to do something completely foreign to all we would consider reasonable and rational. That's why he's God. He's sovereign. It's his world, and he gets to make all the rules—and he gets to bypass our logic and order and do the unexpected whenever it suits his plans best. As C. S. Lewis's character Mr. Beaver says in *The Lion, The Witch and the Wardrobe*, "He isn't safe. But He's good."[1]

A few years ago I had my life neatly laid out; I was certain that God was going to continue to use me to speak and minister primarily to my fellow pastors' wives and to other women. I loved writing and teaching Bible studies to the women of our church and really connected with other pastors' wives at our annual church health conferences. I was happy on the meaningful path where God had placed me.

Then I read a magazine article about HIV&AIDs in Africa and the ensuing orphan crisis. God blew up my happy path and changed the trajectory of my life forever. I morphed from a stay-at-home mom, Bible-study-leading pastor's wife to a travel-the-world global advocate for people living with HIV and the 163,000 orphans in our world, calling local churches to be fresh expressions of the hands and feet of Jesus. God used my SHAPE in ways I could never have anticipated.

I adapted to walking on this new path and grew to love it passionately. Then Matthew died, and the path blew up again, only this time it felt as if I had gotten blown up along with the path. Slowly, painfully, I'm learning how God will use this horrible new life experience as his hands lovingly shape me into the person he desires me to become. I'm confident over time I will become an even more effective minister of his grace and goodness as *all* of who I am—the gifts and abilities I've been given, the passions that drive me, the personality that defines me, the decisions I've made, and the things that have happened to me—come together in a way that honors Jesus.

God is so very good, and I trust him with who I am. You can trust him with who he's shaping you to become as well.

5

Helping Your Children
Survive and Thrive

What if, sometimes, there be mists and fogs so
thick that I cannot see the path? It is enough that
you hold my hand, and guide me in the darkness;
for walking with you in the gloom is far sweeter
and safer than walking alone in the sunlight!

SUSANNAH SPURGEON,
wife of Charles Spurgeon

On August 25, 1979, an adorable, nine-pound-one-ounce
baby girl made me a mommy and changed my life forever. We named her Amy Rebecca—our "beloved little lamb."
Because she was such a big baby and I delivered her the old-fashioned way—no epidural—my body felt every contraction
and every second of the agony of labor.

Later in a postdelivery joyous daze, I took a soothing sitz bath to start the healing process for my bruised and torn body. Suddenly, stark terror supplanted euphoria as the enormity of the responsibility of raising this baby girl crashed over me. The Bible says that children are a gift from the Lord, but at that moment I wanted him to take the gift back. I had done my best to prepare to be a mother, but when Amy was placed in my arms and I looked into her little face, I knew I was in over my head and destined for failure. I cried out to God because I didn't know anybody else big enough to give me answers. Little did I know that was to be the first of thousands of desperate prayers I would pray over the decades—not because she was that difficult but because I needed that much wisdom.

Thirty-seven years, two more precious children (Josh and Matthew), and five grandkids later, I've learned a lot about family and relationships. Raising children is a challenging responsibility. Raising children in a ministry home adds layers of complexity. As ministry couples, we have to think about some things other people don't, including the greatest stressor: raising kids while our congregations observe and evaluate our every move.

Most good parents read at least a couple of books in their search for wisdom on raising the little human beings in their care. I was anxious and probably read more than my share. But the books rarely agreed on how to actually *be* a good parent. It seemed as if the advice was contradictory and often guilt producing. All I knew was I just wanted to do it "right."

Over time—for my own sanity if nothing else—I condensed everything I had read or heard about parenting into three goals.

So whether or not I was the kind of mom who made raisin faces in the oatmeal (I'm not artsy) or remembered to put money under their pillows in the guise of the Tooth Fairy (we renamed ours Flora the Forgetful Tooth Fairy for an obvious reason), I had a game plan.

Here are my three irreducible minimums for raising clergy kids:

1. Let them know God loves them unconditionally.
2. Let them grow through all the stages.
3. Let them go to become mature and independent.

We may get a lot of things wrong as parents, but it's essential we get these three right.

Let Them Know God Loves Them Unconditionally

The number one task of *any* parent is to let children know God loves them unconditionally—wholeheartedly, completely, and without qualifications, limitations, or restrictions. God openly conveys this kind of love for us:

> In this act we see what real love is: it is not our love for God but his love for us. (1 John 4:10 TLB)

> The LORD appeared to us in the past, saying: "I have loved you with an everlasting love; I have drawn you with unfailing kindness." (Jer. 31:3)

> "Though the mountains be shaken
> and the hills be removed,

> yet my unfailing love for you will not be shaken
> nor my covenant of peace be removed,"
> says the Lord, who has compassion on you.
> (Isa. 54:10)

Our primary responsibility, then, is to convey to our kids there is a God who loved them before they even knew he existed. A God whose love is unlike any other love they will ever experience. A God whose love is bottomless, unchanging, and unshakable. A God whose love doesn't vary based on their performance or how good they are. A God whose love isn't influenced by how well-liked they are by others or how successful they are. They need to know in the depths of their souls that this magnificent God freely loves them.

> Our primary **responsibility**, then, is to convey to our kids there is a God who loved them *before* they even knew he existed.

God's love is the secure place to anchor our souls. In light of that, we must teach our kids to continually run to God but particularly in three specific circumstances: when everything is going well and they're happy; when they don't know what to do and have doubts, confusion, and questions; and when they fail, make mistakes, or blatantly sin. In other words, in every single moment of their lives they need to run *to* God, not *away from* God.

When life is going well for our kids—they're healthy and thriving in school, at home, in their relationships, and with the Lord—they need to know that God is the author of every good gift and worthy of their gratitude and appreciation. They can run to him a thousand times a day with prayers of thanks, love, gratitude, and dependence. Teach them that he wants to be their constant companion and that he is as close as their next breath. Building intimacy and familiarity in the good times makes it easier to remember who God is when the harder times come.

There are seasons when kids are confused, unsure of themselves, or in pain due to a loss or a circumstance beyond their control, times when what seemed permanent or stable suddenly isn't anymore. A friendship ends due to conflict or a move; school is a struggle or a constant battle; finances get tight and they're aware of the stress that creates; they don't make the team in a sport they love; a favorite pet dies; they face a challenging decision and feel ill-equipped to make a choice; there's conflict in the church and they feel the fallout; they encounter injustice and can't figure out how a God of love could allow such a broken world to exist. Life, with its never-ending parade of change and upheaval, can be really rough on kids—especially kids who are already dealing with the extra tension of living in the limelight.

Teach them to run to God in these painful, confusing, and uncertain moments. Let them know he is the one stable and secure person in their lives. Let them know he not only cares about them but also will actually show up and give them comfort, guidance, and strength to face hard times. Let them know he's a God they can wrestle with, that it's okay as preachers' kids to have questions and doubts and uncertainties. Let them know it's normal not to have faith and life all figured out. It's all right for life to be messy and not always make sense. They don't have to put everything into neat little boxes with a bow on top. Teach them there aren't always quick and easy answers to the questions that have baffled theologians for millennia. Remind them that the central part of faith is trusting even when they can't figure it all out.

Perhaps the toughest and yet most important time for them to run to God is when they've blown it—when they've failed miserably. Let them know they can run to him when sinful choices and decisions come back to haunt them, perhaps leaving them with life-altering consequences. Our clergy kids desperately need to know that he is a God of second chances and is incredibly merciful, gracious, and forgiving. They feel intense pressure to please us, to not be an embarrassment to us, to not cause trouble for us. Most kids feel this way about their parents, but clergy kids have an extra layer of pressure not to dishonor their pastor dads and moms.

The pattern of running away from the authority figures in our lives when we're in trouble or we've done something wrong is established early in life. How many times have you tried to catch your toddler as he tries to outrun you after you found him doing something he shouldn't be doing? His chubby little legs pump at warp speed when he's trying to escape his messes. Unfortunately, many of us act the same way with God when we think we've done something wrong or think he's going to punish us. We pull a Jonah and run in the opposite direction as fast as our chubby little legs will go. Our task as parents is to keep reinforcing the need to run *to* God when our kids blow it.

Here's the bottom line: our kids will know God's love is unconditional, unmerited, undeserved, and without limitation primarily by the way we love God and the way we love them. God has structured human relationships in such a way that we become the chief conveyor to our children of who God is. As they grow up, our children are going to be heavily influenced—positively and negatively—by school teachers, Sunday school teachers, neighbors, family members, peers, coaches, and other adults they admire. But we have to set the example for them. We are the primary witnesses to the absolute trustworthiness and unconditional love of God. As such, we shape not only their life skills and patterns but their faith as well.

That brings up the gigantic pink elephant in the room—the painful truth we'd rather ignore: if they don't see these truths lived out in our relationships with God or they don't see these truths lived out in our relationships with them, then none of our grand speeches, flannel-graph family devotions, or inspirational talks will matter. We're just blowing smoke in the wind. We're the proverbial hypocrites who talk a big talk but can't walk the walk. Even worse, we trivialize and neutralize the magnificent love God has for our beloved sons and daughters, making it harder for them to build a vibrant life of faith. That's crushing news, because that's never our intent; none of us want to make it tougher for our children to find and know God. We all want to be like the people mentioned in Proverbs 20:7: "God-loyal people, living honest lives, make it much easier for their children" (Message).

This painful reality leads us to ask some hard questions: How will my kids know that God is present in the times of abundance and plenty when it seems as if nothing could ever disturb the tranquility of our home unless they see me quick to express gratitude to God on a daily basis? How will my kids know that God wants to be their rock, their fortress, their strength, their deliverer, their strong tower unless they see me run to God in times of distress, sadness, confusion, grief, and pain? How will they know that God is a second-chance God unless they see me repenting and confessing my own sin and then savoring the grace that allows me to start again?

And here's the second part of the equation. In addition to regularly witnessing our strong, healthy, ever-deepening relationships with God, our kids need to see the same principles at work in our relationships with them, most vitally in the way we handle their doubts and their sins.

It doesn't really matter how many times we tell our children that God is a second-chance God full of grace and mercy—that he is someone to run *to* not *from* no matter what—if we have difficulty showing empathy and compassion in regard to their doubts, and forgiveness, mercy, and grace in regard to their immaturity, sin, and failures. They will likely grow up believing God doesn't love them the same on every given day no matter how they perform or don't perform, and he is the last person they will seek out when they doubt or are fearful, anxious, or guilty. In their deepest struggles, we can be the bridge to their heavenly Father by the way we patiently, gently, and repeatedly emotionally connect with them.

When Josh was a teenager, he confessed that he had used our credit card to buy lunch for his friends on multiple occasions, being devious enough to look at our credit card statements to identify restaurants we frequented so he would have plausible deniability. He told me he had also stolen money from our wallets. He was genuinely repentant and cried huge tears of shame and remorse. My first thought was, *You've violated my trust, broken my heart, and when I'm through crying, I'm going to get up from here and kill you.* My second thought was, *God, what do I say in this moment? I understand this is a pivotal moment in Josh's life. The way I handle this failure may make or break his relationships with you and with me.*

I put aside my thoughts of murder and looked at my son, shattered with remorse, and said through my tears, "I am shocked to the core. I'm so sad you have deceived us and stolen from us. I'm deeply hurt to think you took advantage of our love and trust. But I love you fiercely, and nothing can ever change my love for you as my child. I forgive you. I know you despise yourself right now and think you are dirt in God's eyes, but God loves you even more than I do. We're going to run to God together right now. I want you to confess what you've done and ask for his mercy because his forgiveness is even greater than mine. And we're going to pray together on our knees and ask him to restore our broken relationship." And we did. Just recently, Josh told me it was an unforgettable experience. Knowing for certain that not only God but also Rick and I would forgive him gave him enormous comfort and encouragement. The ending of the story is that Josh is now responsible for the oversight of all of our finances. The young man who used his intelligence to creatively deceive us now uses his creativity and intelligence for our good.

From infancy, Matthew was a very sensitive boy who felt things passionately. As he grew, he began to show signs of mental illness. By the age of seven, he was depressed, was having panic attacks, and was diagnosed with ADHD. At eleven, he was diagnosed with early onset bipolar disorder. Over the years OCD, suicidal ideation, major depressive disorder, body dysmorphic disorder, and borderline personality disorder all became a part of the lexicon of his life; it seemed as if every doctor visit included a new diagnosis. Even so, he loved Jesus and gave his life to him at an early age. I still have the notes he took at various camps and retreats and even the notes he took on his dad's sermons—very tender stuff. And yet, as he navigated through adolescence, his faith began to waver as he wrestled with how a God of love could allow so much suffering in his life. We agonized with him when he wondered why he had OCD, which interfered with his ability to differentiate between the Holy Spirit and the voices in his head. He eventually openly questioned God—sometimes angrily and with great frustration. Obviously, his actions could have reflected poorly on us as his parents, leading church members to suspect our qualifications to lead the church. I'm sure there were a few people along the way who decided we must be terribly off track to have a son who struggled so intensely, but we realized he was ill and there was no shame in having a mentally ill child. We wept with him and for him and learned to just listen to his pain; logical "answers" were not helpful. While we did our best to protect his privacy, his struggles were no secret to anyone who was paying attention.

Your child might have committed a terrible sin that broke your heart, your daughter might have a mental illness, or your son might let it be known that he has doubts about the whole Christianity thing—and you face a powerful dilemma as a ministry family. Should you hide the truth or acknowledge that you are like every other family in the church—imperfect, broken saints in need of God's rescue and mercy? Don't let the pressure to appear perfect and whole cause you to create shame in your children. I believe your first responsibility is to the children God has given to you. I don't know if you realize it or not, but how you handle their doubts, confusion, pain, weaknesses, and even illnesses becomes a predictor of how you will respond to the same issues in your congregation.

It hurts when you realize your kids aren't getting the messages you intended to provide. There are factors you can't always control in your kids—mental illness being one of them—but one major roadblock to giving clear and consistent messages is that you can never pass on to someone else something you haven't experienced yourself. David Seamands writes in *Healing for Damaged Emotions*:

> Many years ago I was driven to the conclusion that the two major causes of emotional problems among evangelical Christians are these: The failure to understand, receive and live out God's unconditional grace and forgiveness. And the failure to give out that unconditional love and forgiveness and grace to other people. We read, we hear, we believe a good theology of grace. But that's not how we live. We believe grace in our heads but not in our gut level feelings or in our relationships. It's all on a head level. The good news of the gospel of grace has not penetrated to the level of our emotions.[1]

You may need to do some business with God. Perhaps you are aware in the deepest place in your heart that you have yet to really accept and *feel* that you are loved and accepted by God and that he sees you as someone who is covered by the blood of Jesus.

These messages of unconditional love, mercy, and grace are communicated not just in the moments of crises but in the day-to-day interactions within a family: doing chores, at the grocery store, driving to school, cooking dinner, folding laundry. Some of our most powerful teaching times happen as we walk through life together. But here's the catch. We actually have to *be there* for these moments to occur.

Robert Reich, former secretary of labor in President Bill Clinton's first administration, resigned his position in the cabinet to be with his family. He said:

> I don't know very much about teen-age girls, but teen-age boys are like clam shells: hard on the outside, but when they open up for an instant, and they only open up for an instant, you can see the beauty and the vulnerability inside, and sometimes you get a quick peek at an absolute pearl. But you can't predict exactly when they will open up. And if you're not there when they do—it's often two or three o'clock in the morning, but you don't know—you might as well be on the moon.[2]

The only way to see those "pearls" is to be there.

This is where it all starts. Anything else I'm going to say about helping our kids survive and thrive while living in the fishbowl is small potatoes compared to helping them know God loves them unconditionally. Nothing else they ever learn—nothing—will affect them as dramatically or as foundationally as this certainty.

——— Let Them Grow through All the Stages ———

Our children are going to grow through stages, and they need people farther along on the road of life who can lay out a consistent and reliable path for them to run on. As the Lord says in Deuteronomy 32:46, "Be sure to obey all these commands that I have given you today. Repeat them to your children, so that they may faithfully obey all of God's teachings" (GNT). God instructs parents to be the road warriors, the trailblazers—the ones with the machetes in hand, slashing the brush to create the trail for them to follow. The Bible says in Hebrews 12:13,

"Mark out a straight, smooth path for your feet so that those who follow you, though weak and lame, will not fall and hurt themselves but become strong" (TLB). We need to create a path that is so honest and sure they will not stumble and fall on it as they follow us. Hopefully, we will create a path that leads directly to God and his truth.

Our kids are going to grow, and the way they grow is through stages. Have you ever had a mom moment when you looked at your child and thought, "Holy moley! Who are you and when did you get so tall?" It happens in the blink of an eye. That's why books such as *What to Expect When You're Expecting* and *What to Expect the First Year* are so popular. They recognize that children grow and develop in fairly predictable stages, and the books demystify the process for us.

There are at least four ways children grow through stages:

- physically
- socially
- sexually
- spiritually

While I'm not going to go into the ways children grow physically, I do want to share a few things I've learned about how living in a ministry family impacts the way they grow socially, sexually, and spiritually.

Let Them Grow Socially

Every child grows socially, and the important role of friends and peers increases through their development. Unfortunately, it won't take very long for your children to decide your opinion doesn't matter nearly as much as that of their friends. Even if they respect you, by the time they reach adolescence, your opinion will have dropped way down the totem pole.

When Amy was five and starting kindergarten, I bought her a pair of sturdy, burgundy leather shoes. I intended those shoes to last the entire school year. But a few weeks after school started, the burgundy shoes disappeared. I was completely mystified by their disappearance and asked Amy, "What happened to your shoes? Where could they be?" "I don't know, Mommy. I don't know where they are." We searched the house, we searched our cars, we searched out in the yard. We searched every place we could think of. No luck. She kept protesting, "Mommy, I don't know where they are." I was a naïve first-time mom, and I believed her. The child had to have shoes, so I bought her a pair of Jellies—cheap plastic shoes that were the rage of her kindergarten class—to tide her over until we could locate the leather shoes.

Her "sin" eventually found her out. Many months later as I was helping her clean her room, we moved her little doll bed, and lo and behold, there were her shoes. We were both surprised—she had forgotten where she had hidden them. Turns out she had "lost" them because some girls at school had made fun of those shoes; evidently, sturdy leather shoes were not as cool as Jellies to the kindergarten fashion police. Amy lied to me for months because my opinion didn't matter nearly as much as her friends' opinions.

I had no clue that sturdy, burgundy leather shoes versus fluorescent, plastic Jellies was just the opening volley in the struggle between peer pressure and my desires for my daughter. I quickly learned in light of the vast array of issues I could fight with her about that it was good to remember the age-old parenting advice: choose wisely the hills you're prepared to die on. Battles are looming, clergy households included. Particularly clergy households. Which of those battles are you ready to fight to the death for? Which hills are you ready to die on?

In the hippie days of our youth, short, neatly trimmed hair went out of style and girls *and* guys began to wear their hair long. Rick started growing his curly blond hair out, and his pastor didn't like it. He thought Rick was making some sort of a political statement with his long hair. He made fun of Rick and said rude things to him. Rick's theologically and politically conservative parents could have decided this was a hill to die on, but Rick's dad's response was, "Grow it while you can, because one of these days you won't have any hair on your head!" Even though the spiritual climate was one of disapproval, his dad decided it was not something worth fighting over and let it go.

God does not look at our kids the way we do. He does not look at their hair or the clothes they wear. He does not look at whether they have an earring or a tattoo or whatever currently represents coolness. God looks at something far more significant. First Samuel 16:7 says, "God does not see the same way people see. People look at the outside of a person, but the LORD looks at the heart" (NCV).

This aspect of parenting has an added edge because we are raising our kids—and figuring out what battles to fight—in front of a watching world. Often we're okay with the ways our kids are growing socially, but the elder or deacon board is not. This can create a lot of tension and stress as we balance the needs of our children with the opinions of the elders or the board. What is acceptable is such an individual standard, but my two cents is this: say yes to your children whenever possible and save your energy and strength for the battles that really matter.

So let your kids grow through the social stages. Don't freak out easily. What they are doing is normal and to be expected. What's that British slogan? Keep calm and carry on.

Let Them Grow Sexually

We come into this world recognized by our sex, although routine prenatal ultrasounds can reveal whether we're a boy or a girl long before we emerge from the safety of the womb. But there's more to sexuality than our sex. Our identity is tied up in our sexuality and therefore critical to who we are as persons. Entire books have been written about talking to your kids about sex and sexuality, so I'm not going to pretend I'm an expert in this department. I will pass on a few of the aspects I have found to be the most beneficial in helping children grow sexually.

Some of you can just skip these next couple of paragraphs because you've got this one—you grew up with healthy attitudes about sex, your parents modeled a healthy relationship, your marriage is healthy, and you never struggled personally with sex or sexuality. Talking to your kids about sex is the same as talking about baseball or ballet. Hooray for you and your kids! You're the lucky ones. For some of you, though, this is a tough area of conversation with your kids, and you definitely dread "the talk." You've already read part of my story. I lived with sexual brokenness, so you can imagine I needed a whole lot of inner healing to help my kids grow sexually.

For reasons I've never entirely figured out, my sweet mom could hardly say the word *sex* let alone have an in-depth conversation with me about it. She stammered and sputtered as if *sex* had about ten s's in front of it: s-s-s-s-s-s-s-sex. We laugh about it now, but back then, whew! It was hard for her. When my parents determined it was time to have "the talk" with me, they pulled out a large, brightly illustrated children's encyclopedia and opened it up to the page that talked about the birds and the bees. I kid you not. The birds and the bees. They sat me down and pointed to the pictures that showed how bees pollinate flowers. There were vague, veiled references to men, women, and babies, but they were embarrassed and I was embarrassed and I recall being *so* relieved when they closed the book and said we were finished. Somehow I was supposed to extrapolate from the nature lesson that this had something to do with human sexuality and me. It was all very confusing and awkward. Clearly, I didn't grow up with parents who were comfortable with sex and sexuality.

When our kids came along, it helped that Rick had not received the sexually repressed messages I had. I didn't always get it right, but I made a real effort to learn and grow so I could talk to my kids in a much more natural way than my parents had talked to me. I'll never forget the day I realized I had done pretty well with this whole "be comfortable" approach. I was driving Amy to school when she was about fifteen, and she said, "Mom, what is . . . ?" and asked a very intimate sexual question. To be honest, there was a split second when I nearly drove off the road because until that moment the car ride had been a typical sleepy, half-awake, early morning school run. But I took a deep breath and said in a matter-of-fact voice, "Well, that is . . ." and I fully explained the answer to her question. She yawned and said, "Okay. That's fine." After I dropped her off at school, I thought to myself how that question would have freaked my mother out and sent our car rolling into the ditch. I mentally patted myself on the back. "Good job, Mama," I said to my only marginally freaked-out self. "You're making progress."

I wish talking about sex and sexuality was as relatively simple today as it was when I was small or even when my children were growing through the stages. It's not, though, and parents need to be well-equipped and ready to talk about absolutely everything related to sex. No question or topic should be off-limits. Of course, I believe it is primarily the parents' responsibility to do this and do it well, but the church must be an additional strong and positive resource that affirms the values and messages we teach in our homes. Our homes and our churches should be the best sources of loving, accurate, and factual information about sex. If not, we leave our kids vulnerable to messages from external sources that aren't as reliable or won't reinforce biblical values. Our kids need strong, positive messages about their bodies and their changing and maturing sexuality, not just messages about responsible and godly sexual behavior, although those are critical too. We have the amazing opportunity to give them credible and reasonable answers to their questions and to show them how living for Jesus is possible in a sex-saturated culture. (There are some suggested resources at the end of the book.)

Another way to help our kids grow sexually is to be physically affectionate with them. It's impossible to overemphasize the value of hugging, kissing, and patting them on the shoulder or arm—all the appropriate touches that express deep love and value. There's probably nothing quite like physical touch that lets somebody know they are of inestimable worth.

You might protest that you weren't raised in a family in which you were shown much physical affection and don't really know how to do that very well. You might have more of an uphill challenge than someone raised in an emotionally warm home—but you can learn. Don't let your children grow up without the benefit of being touched and hugged and kissed and told how much they are loved and how much you love to be with them.

When Josh was fifteen, he went away for a week of camp with our youth group. I fully expected that when I picked him up he would toss a casual "Oh, hi Mom" in my direction. Instead, he ran over and gave me a huge hug. Then he took my hand and said, "Mom, I've missed you. I can't wait to tell you all the great things that happened this week." I was amazed that he felt the freedom to publicly express affection to me at that point in adolescence. Some of it was his personality, but some of it was because he had learned how to express affection freely in our home.

A third way to help them grow sexually is to be affectionate with your husband in front of them. Again, so much of what we teach our children is not about what we say. It is about how we behave. You can say, "Yes, it's healthy for husbands and wives to love each other," but the most powerful lesson is seeing parents hugging, kissing, holding hands, and talking affectionately to each other and about each other. It helps create for kids the picture of what marriage can be like.

Rick embarrasses me with his public pronouncements about how pretty he thinks I am. He has done this since we first met. He loves it when I walk into a room he's already in and he (in his always Tigger-ish way) exclaims, "I am hopelessly in love with this woman!" It doesn't matter whether there are ten people or one hundred people in the room—doesn't bother him at all. And of course, my introverted self is mortified to have one hundred sets of eyes on me, but he's done it for forty-one years, and he's not likely to stop any time soon. My kids comment about how often they have heard their dad—in public and in private—talk about how much he loves me. I think it has set the bar high for them to create good marriages for themselves.

Let Them Grow Spiritually

The most important spiritual lesson we can pass on to our kids is that God loves them unconditionally, but there's one more thought.

As our children pass through the stages of their spiritual development, we gradually want to transition them from parent-controlled decisions to self-controlled decisions and ultimately to God-controlled decisions.

We start by controlling everything about our kids' lives. Initially, we decide what they eat, what time they eat, what they wear, where they can go, what activities they will participate in, what school they will attend—we make every decision with little input from them.

As they mature, we give away some of the control so they can begin to make decisions for themselves. But that's not the end goal. We have to help them understand that their decision-making process must really be based on what God wants for them, not merely on what they want for themselves or what they perceive we want for them. For pastors' kids, it's especially crucial they learn not to make decisions based on what Mom and Dad will think. We guide them as they grow spiritually to ask themselves, "What does God say about this?" This is a process, and it doesn't come quickly. And the hardest part? They'll make so many mistakes. And we have to let them go to become mature and proficient in controlling their own lives, even when they are making choices we don't fully support.

Sometimes letting go happens in beautiful moments when our kids get married or go off to college. We're so proud of where they are in life and what they're achieving. We have raised them to leave us and live as independent men and women who love and serve God. It's poignant, but it's good.

Sometimes our kids head off in directions that break our hearts, and letting go is accompanied by sadness, disappointment, and fear. There are times we have to let go in ways we desperately don't want to. All of this becomes much, much harder if mental illness, physical illness, traumatic experiences, and grief need to be factored in. For children and teens who have these added layers of stress and pain, different approaches are required, ones that don't focus as much on "tough love" as on parent/child emotional connection and attachment. (Check out the resource section for more information.)

But for kids who aren't living with one of these challenges, repeated wrong choices and decisions often leave parents feeling wounded by their behavior and worried for their future. By leaving our values and ideals, it feels as though they are leaving *us* too. You know pastors' families are not immune to this; many of you love a prodigal son or daughter and live with a heavy heart.

Luke 15 records Jesus's well-known parable of the prodigal son. When the prodigal son leaves home, he leaves not only his father but also all that is good and right in his life. He abandons his training, his values, and his relationships. The father lets him go to become responsible for his own choices, to make mistakes.

You know the story. The son makes a complete mess of his life and ends up living in a pigpen—a place no Jewish boy should ever be. The father does not go to his son in the pigpen and say, "Let me make it more comfortable for you. I've got some soft fur to line the pigpen so you won't be bothered by the mud and the smell of the pigs." The father doesn't do that. Due to his unrelieved misery, the prodigal son eventually comes to his senses and returns home where he belongs.

What a lesson for us when our kids are making choices we feel are wrong and are harmful for them. If we "fur line the pigpen," we could potentially keep our kids from coming to their senses. This is one of the toughest dilemmas for us as parents. We want to protect our kids from making mistakes. When they're about to fall, it's natural to want to cushion the blow so they don't get hurt. But that's not the way they mature. Henri Nouwen says, "[Our children] do not belong to us. They belong to God, and one of the greatest acts of trust in God is letting our children make their own choices and find their own way."[3]

At some point, we stop being responsible *for* our children and start becoming responsible *to* our children. Galatians 6:5 says "For we are each responsible for our own conduct" (NLT). The transition from being responsible *for* to being responsible *to* is a tough one. None of us want our children to make mistakes they will pay for the rest of their lives. On the other hand, we cannot always control their decisions, and we must stop trying to. The very best way we can love our prodigals *in certain circumstances* is to let the natural consequences fall where they may—not out of anger or bitterness or vindictiveness but with the dearest hope that the relationship will be restored.

Hebrews 12:11 says, "At the time discipline is not much fun. It always feels like it's going against the grain. But later of course it pays off handsomely for it is the well trained who find themselves mature in their relationship with God" (Message). You became a mature woman of God because you made mistakes, errors, and some wrong choices. In that process, you learned from the mistakes as you reaped the consequences. Somewhere along the way you decided you didn't want to live that way anymore. So you decided to make a different set of decisions, and from that different set of decisions you became a spiritually mature woman. We have to let our kids go through the *process* so they can have the *product*—spiritual maturity.

Commitments

As we close this particular conversation, I invite you to make some parenting commitments. These decisions will go a long way in helping your kids not just survive but thrive in the ministry.

Commit to letting your children know that God loves them unconditionally and that you do too. If you do nothing else besides create a home where grace and mercy reign, you will have accomplished something incredible.

Commit to letting them grow through the stages without panicking. Don't hesitate to ask other people for input and insight. Don't hesitate to admit you're having some troubles with your kids and don't know what to do. Don't be afraid to ask for help.

Commit to letting them go to become the people God wants them to be, even if it causes pain to them and to you in the process. Trust God to write the future for your children.

6

Sharing Your Life

What the Lord wants is, that you shall go about
the business to which He sets you, not asking
for an easy post, nor grumbling at a hard one.

CATHERINE BOOTH,
wife of William Booth

When my dad was in seminary in the 1950s, the accepted wisdom of the day was, "Don't seek close friends in the church; it will create jealousy." A part of me completely understands that thinking—especially since most churches in America have less than two hundred members and everybody knows everybody else's business. The sad part, though, is that this approach can lead to great loneliness and isolation.

My parents were also extremely careful about how much they shared with church members about the challenges, struggles, and pain they experienced. They were taught to talk about only the positive parts of life and faith, not the burdens, doubts, or broken parts. My father didn't talk about his first marriage—ever. I can't count the number of sermons he preached on marriage in his fifty-plus years in ministry, but not once did he mention the personal sting of divorce. When my younger brother was a heroin addict and in jail for shoplifting to support his habit, they carried the burden and sorrow mostly by themselves. A few people who had become lifelong friends were compassionate and prayerful, but my parents didn't share their heartache about my brother with their congregation.

Some of you are nodding your heads as you read because you received the same advice: don't get too close to church members; keep your problems to yourself; don't share deeply.

But let's be honest. Isn't part of the reason we don't share our real selves and our real problems because we're too embarrassed? Don't we agonize over what other people would think of us if they knew? The Bible calls us out on our habit of hiding our sins, weaknesses, and failures. John 3:19 says, "This is the verdict: Light has come into the world, but people loved darkness instead of light because their deeds were evil."

I'm fascinated by roly-poly bugs and always think of them when I read this verse. If I pick up a rock in my garden and expose these prehistoric-looking creatures to the sun, they fall off the rock they've been clinging to and curl into a tight ball or scurry for another hiding place. They prefer the darkness.

Isn't that an apt description of our modus operandi? We cover and hide our sins, our failures, our brokenness, our weaknesses, our temptations, dreading the exposure of light that reveals what we work so hard to cover up. As we grow more proficient in hiding, we become as Paul David Tripp says, totally blind to our own blindness.[1] This thought recently occurred to me in a moment of clarity: My ideal self is so much nicer than my real self. My ideal self is so much more spiritual than my real self. My ideal self is so much more loving than my real self. My ideal self is so much wiser than my real self. My ideal self is so much kinder than my real self. Who I think I am and who I really am are frequently at odds with each other. As a result, I hide out in the darkness of pretense. This is tragic—completely unnecessary and unbiblical—but it has become our default mode. God has another way. Get off the pedestal, use your own life as an example, and pursue friendship.

Get Off the Pedestal

Edward Bratcher says that one of the greatest temptations and pitfalls for people in ministry is the tendency to try to walk on water:[2] to be all things to all people, know it all, have all the right answers, be certain of how to handle every situation, have solutions for every problem, and pretty much be perfect—less like a human being and more like God. We allow ourselves to be put up on a pedestal of supposed superiority. We belly flop time after time because, of course, we aren't superhuman. But that doesn't stop us from trying, even as we resent and complain about the pressures and expectations from our congregations that put us on a pedestal.

The most truthful thing we can disclose about ourselves is this: our congregations' idealization and idolization feed our egos. We all enjoy being on a pedestal where others can admire us. Who doesn't like to be thought of as someone who has it all together? A sick part of us wants others to believe we're *that good.* "Wow! Look at her—she really knows Jesus! I wish I could be like her!" It's humbling to acknowledge the vile and rotten ego within each of us that responds to being elevated to such a high place.

Growing up in a pastor's home, I was keenly aware that people watched us and judged us as the pastor and his family, putting us on a pedestal of perfection. My parents didn't encourage us to fake it, but they were keenly aware that the gospel can be harmed. In their vigilance to make sure we didn't do anything that would cause harm to the name of Christ, "What will other people think?" became the guiding principle for our family. I dealt with the pressure by going into a self-made box—a place of strict external behavior and attitudes that kept me toeing the line outwardly while hiding my embarrassing failures inwardly.

But as I've told you, I fell apart after Rick and I got married. When our pain exceeded our fears and our shame, we went for marriage counseling. Gratefully, within a few short sessions, I had an experience that altered the course of my marriage, as well as my relationship to God. We came home from a counseling appointment too upset to talk to each other. Rick went to the living room, and I lay on our bed crying with frustration, shame, and a terrible sense of failure. As I lay there staring up at the ceiling, I became aware of something strange happening. I began to experience a sensation of God's love filling every corner of the room. His mercy and grace seemed to hover tangibly around me, completely enveloping and embracing me. It was so real that I thought I could reach out my fingers and actually touch it. For the first time in my life, I could *feel* God's love. I had known of his love since I was a baby, but I had never *felt* it on an emotional level.

I'm not given to visions, but that day I had one. I saw myself as a little butterfly tightly encased in a rigid, unyielding chrysalis. For no apparent reason, the chrysalis suddenly split open and the butterfly shook off the constricting cocoon, opened her wings, and freely flew straight up to the sky.

"That's me! That's me! That's me!" I said, laughing and crying with amazement and joy, delirious in the freedom of God's complete and total acceptance of me. I got it—I really got it. He didn't love me because of what I did for him—all the good girl rules I kept—or hate me because I was irreparably broken. He just loved me as I was.

> When our *pain* exceeded our *fears* and our shame, we went for marriage counseling.

In much the same way that Hagar knew God *saw* her (Gen. 16:13), I knew then that God saw my pain and suffering. He knew about the molestation that had launched such an ugly cycle of sexual brokenness, pornography, and sexual failure in marriage. He knew how hard I had tried, where I'd gotten stuck, and that I didn't know how to get unstuck. He wasn't mad at me or ashamed of me; instead, I felt his embrace of all of me. *God loves me.*

In response to this experiential encounter with God's unconditional love for me, a brand-new inner freedom was born. I took a vow before God in that moment: "I will never go back into the box of perfectionism and pleasing other people again. Never. Never. Never. I'm jumping off the pedestal today, even if I have to stand on the roof of our church building someday and shout to everyone who walks by, 'We are just like you! We're just human beings! We have problems! There are days we don't even know if God exists. Some days we don't like each other. We are just people, and we refuse to stay on the pedestal!'"

God wants you to live in that same grace-filled freedom. He does not want you to get comfortable on that narrow pedestal—in fact, he wants you to climb down off the pedestal *right now*. He does not want you to live in the rigid box of perfectionism and pleasing others. He does not want you to feel as if you are trapped and cannot escape. He does not want you to live with the fear that if anybody really, truly knew, all would be lost. The fact is if any of us knew—really knew all there was to know about one another—we'd never be able to stand to look at one another again. Only God can handle the totality of all there is to know about us and still love us. Yet, his desire is for us to know and be known, and that can happen only when we get down off the pedestal and come out of the box of perfectionism.

People have asked over the years, "What do you think is the secret of Saddleback?" I'm convinced one of the "secrets" of Saddleback is that we started with the intention to be real about ourselves and to invite other broken men and women to join us in this effort to live with transparency. We wanted this to be a place where anyone could say, "I'm broken. I'm messed up. I have hurts, habits, and hang-ups." We wanted to be a congregation who could say with Barnabas and Paul in Acts 14:15, "We are merely human beings—just like you! We have come to bring you the Good News that you should turn from these worthless things and turn to the living God, who made heaven and earth, the sea, and everything in them" (NLT).

God has wired us as relational beings who are meant to live open and authentic lives, walking in the light of fellowship with God and a shared life of love with one another. John tells us, "But if we walk in the light, God himself being the light, we also experience a shared life with one another, as the sacrificed blood of Jesus, God's Son, purges all our sin" (1 John 1:7 Message). When we start being honest about the fact that we're merely human beings, we take our first steps into the light.

Use Your Own Life as an Example

There's always going to be a temptation to go back into the box and not tell your story, but you have a story that's worth telling. You actually encourage other people when you use your own story. Has it ever occurred to you that you are not living your life just for yourself? That the things that happen to you—the things you've gone through and struggled with—are actually meant to encourage others?

My younger brother has been clean and sober for several decades, but for many years he was a heroin and opioid addict. Fairly early in our time at Saddleback, when my brother was still an addict, I was talking to a man I casually knew, and he said, "Even though I've been at Saddleback for some time, I don't really know a lot about you. Do you have siblings?"

I said, "Yes, I have a brother."

"Has he always followed the Lord?"

"No, he has not." I told him about Andy and the hell he was living through.

The man I was chatting with got tears in his eyes and said, "Wow! That's so great!"

His response stunned me into silence, but in my mind I was thinking, *What in the world is wrong with you, you jerk?*

This man was not known for having a high compassion quotient, so his response wasn't too far out of character. But he hurried on to say, "What I mean is it's so comforting to me to know that your family isn't perfect—that you guys have walked through some really hard things. It makes me feel like maybe my family isn't so weird, that my family isn't so strange. To know that your family has also struggled, that your family has dealt with something as terrible as addiction, it gives me hope." If I had lied or pretended or just kept it vague—"Well, you know, my brother's had some struggles"—our talk probably wouldn't have meant a whole lot to this man. But because I was willing to use my life as an example and wasn't fearful that he would think poorly of my family, our encounter allowed him to feel more normal than he had when he had walked into that room.

The apostle Paul says in Philippians 1:12–14 that the false imprisonments and beatings he endured actually emboldened other believers to speak the Word of God more courageously and fearlessly. He understood that by living authentically and transparently he could inspire and encourage others. His life was not his own, nor was it solely for his own benefit. Oswald Chambers says:

> There is no such thing as a private life, or a place to hide in this world, for a man or woman who is intimately aware of and shares in the sufferings of Jesus Christ. God divides the private life of His saints and makes it a highway for the world on one hand and for Himself on the other. No human being can stand that unless he is identified with Jesus Christ. We are not sanctified for

ourselves. We are called into intimacy with the gospel, and things happen that appear to have nothing to do with us. But God is getting us into fellowship with Himself. Let Him have His way. If you refuse, you will be of no value to God in His redemptive work in the world, but will be a hindrance and a stumbling block.[3]

Use your own life as an example for people. It will give them encouragement to come out of their boxes too. It will give them hope.

——— Pursue Friendship ———

How do we as pastors' wives move past our knee-jerk reactions to hide and cover up our real selves? What can we do to get past this major barrier to intimacy? We must practice walking in the light—confess everything to God, receive his continual gift of forgiveness, and then walk in the shared light of his grace with others through friendships.

Here's where this idea gets intensely practical. If you start walking in the light and sharing your real life, people will see your junk. They will know for certain you can't walk on water. They will see the cracks in your marriage and the holes in your faith. They will see the inconsistencies and the hypocrisies. They will see the blind spots that you can't see. They will see you in your worst moments as well as your shining ones. You can't pretend for very long with a friend.

Some of you are saying, "Exactly! This is why I don't share. I don't want people to know my stuff!" The truth

The *truth* is knowing and being known is the only way to last over the long haul in *ministry*.

is knowing and being known is the only way to last over the long haul in ministry. Close relationships are one of the main safeguards that keep us from that terrible syndrome of hiding and pretending we can walk on water. Edward Bratcher says that the only way to get off the pedestal and stop trying to walk on water is to pursue close, intimate friendships.

> One becomes truly human through relationships. Conversely, one cannot become human in isolation. There is no real possibility of the clergy overcoming the temptation to walk on water if they do not develop friends.[4]

I have pursued four types of relationships through the years, with differing levels of intimacy, and I urge you to do the same.

Enjoy Social Relationships

The goal of these friendships is purely social—these are people to hang out with to have fun. These friendships often spring up between neighbors, with those who have kids in the same sport or class at school, or with those who share a hobby. You're not necessarily looking to go deep or walk away with amazing spiritual insights. It's not necessary to solve the world's problems when you're together. In fact, it's actually healthy to have some friendships that don't tax your brain or your problem-solving capacity. With these friends, you relax, kick back, laugh a lot, and enjoy participating in an event or activity together. These people are just fun and easy. The point is not to have a spiritual conversation—although it's always an added bonus—but to unwind and rejuvenate in a lighthearted manner. It's all good.

Draw Strength from a Ministry Support Group

As a pastor's wife, you also need friendships with women who are living the same glass-house life you are, to feel supported by people with a similar life experience. That's because a life in ministry has unique positives and negatives that only those who are living it can understand. It's just like a doctor's wife can understand another doctor's wife, or a military wife can understand another military wife. The unique challenges and experiences have to be lived to be appreciated. As a breast cancer survivor, I can be with women who have had breast cancer and no words are necessary. When I'm with other survivors of suicide loss, we can speak volumes with just our hugs. It's like saying, "I get it. I hear you." It is always so encouraging to me to instantly feel a bond with another pastor's wife that goes beyond denominational or cultural differences. Don't you love it when you make a comment about your life and another pastor's wife excitedly says, "You feel that way? I do too. That's exactly what it's like for me."

One of the common complaints about a life in ministry is that it can be lonely. Yes, it can. Especially if you subscribe to the point of view that says you can't have friends. But a life in ministry doesn't automatically have to be lonely.

Many years ago one brave pastor's wife in our area sent an invitation to about twenty-five other pastors' wives who lived in the Saddleback Valley and invited them to come to her house for lunch. Probably twenty showed up the first day, and she talked to us about her desire to be with other women who had a measure of understanding of what her life and family were like. She invited us to get together four times a year, and while about half of the original women dropped out pretty quickly, a small group of us decided to try it. For the next four years, we got together once a quarter either at someone's home or at a restaurant. We made a pact not to talk about our churches in a specific way. Obviously, we were all in ministry, but the church sizes and styles varied widely, so we focused on talking about ourselves and our families—not comparing church programs or church events. The couples even got together a few times over the years, and in the early years of Saddleback, when I was figuring out my role, this group of women was a source of emotional strength for me.

This is within the reach of most of us. If you don't know where to begin, look on the internet and find the addresses of churches within a five- to ten-mile radius of your church and start sending out invitations. Only a few women might respond, but those few will be grateful, and you just might discover a new friend.

From the early days of Saddleback, I also sought to connect with the wives of pastors as they were hired. There was one, and then two, and then three. We got together for breakfast on a Saturday morning every few months at my house or an inexpensive restaurant. There was no program or strategy or plan. I just knew I needed peer support and figured they did too. Because we got to know one another, some of the unavoidable friction that can occur between staff members was minimized. We weren't strangers to one another and actually cared about one another's lives.

Because Saddleback has a large number of pastors and younger men on a ministerial education track, my sister-in-love, Chaundel Holladay, has taken the wives of these men under her wing. I think by the last count (it seems to change weekly) she was shepherding over one hundred women. She essentially pastors a small church. Many of these women are new in ministry or newly married; it would be easy for them to get lost in the shuffle. For decades now, we have encouraged these women to attend three events a year designed exclusively for them: a Christmas party, a weekend retreat, and an end-of-summer pool party where 99 percent of the women don't get in the pool. The women are put into smaller groups of eight to ten ministers' wives for year-round fellowship and caregiving. Chaundel also started an invitation-only Facebook page where we communicate with one another; support one another; and alert one another to news of births, illnesses, prayer requests, and, most importantly, who's having a garage sale that weekend! It takes an enormous amount of work for her and her small planning team to keep up with these women, but it's worth it. I've always believed that when the wives feel connected to one another and have a safe place to vent, cry, ask questions, serve, and be prayed for, they experience more satisfaction in their role as a pastor's wife and are happier overall.

You can modify these ideas to fit your circumstances. If you're it—you're the only pastor's wife in your church—get together with other pastors' wives in your area. If there are other pastors' wives in your church, meet occasionally to build friendships and benefit from peer support. If you're in a larger church, consider what you or a team of pastors' wives can do to help the new or young pastors' wives find the peer support and encouragement they need for life in ministry. Don't let loneliness be the norm.

Live Life in Community through a Small Group

Rick and I have been in the same couples' small group for fifteen years. I've been in several women's small groups through the years—and loved them—and we tried several other couples' groups that didn't quite work out. But this group . . . I hardly have words. Just thinking about them makes me weepy. We have made a commitment to one another that is almost as unbreakable as marriage vows. Until death separates us, we plan to go through life together. It is so precious to me to know there are people who love me to that depth. There's such safety and comfort and security with these brothers and sisters committed to my well-being. We have already lived together through almost every conceivable painful life experience: financial stress, cancer, mental illness, heart attacks, deaths of parents and siblings, suicide, serious marriage problems, conflict, disability of a child, depression, adoption, and so many others.

My small group fills so many of the "I need close friends" boxes, but I also believe some of my core issues will never be resolved without this group. Rick has worked on me for more than forty-one years—bless his heart. He's about shot his wad. There are just some parts of my personality and character that aren't going to change. There are some parts of his personality that I've tried to work my magic on to no avail. I've used all my words on him. He's used all his words on me. But in the warm, accepting circle of our small group, they have permission to say things to me I can't hear from him. They can say things to him he can't hear from me. I am convinced I will not become the person God intends for me to be without this group of people.

Larry Crabb calls this kind of friendship the safest place on earth. He says:

> Has anyone ever actually witnessed the contortions my soul sometimes goes through? Whom do I trust enough to be my confessor, to see up close the blood that spills during my spiritual battles, the cowardly retreats I sometimes take, the fears that occasionally paralyze me? If the answer is no one, then do all the words of encouragement I hear have no more power than the sentimental poetry inside greeting cards? Am I to lose my personal privacy so that a few people can speak deeply into a battle they understand?[5]

You may not be in that kind of small group. You may not be in any small group at this moment, but I urge you to seriously consider joining a group if possible. The intimacy, support, and strength gained from a group of people committed to your personal well-being over the long haul can be so life giving, and even life saving.

Find One or Two Soul Mates for Sustenance

The deepest level of friendship is with those whose love feeds our souls. It's likely you won't have many of these relationships over a lifetime. Some of you have had the same best friend since childhood, while others can say several of these nourishing relationships came at the exact right moment, stayed for a season, and then somehow lessened. You really just need one or two friends at a time who truly understand you. Such a friend can speak into your life with complete freedom because you know in the depths of your being she is for you. She will tell you the truth about you. This rare friend goes the last 10 percent in a conversation, saying the things no one else is willing to say. She can correct you, lovingly (though sometimes her tone is strong) calling you on the carpet while remaining your cheerleader. She believes in you and God's call on your life; she affirms your gifts; and she prays fervently for your spiritual growth and maturity. Everybody needs a few friends with sustaining love.

In 1 Samuel, David was in a tough spot; King Saul was chasing him, trying to kill him. David was living on the run, never knowing from day to day if he would survive. Saul's son, Jonathan—David's dearest friend—put his own life at risk by going on a search for David. Jonathan wasn't afraid to identify with David and to show up in his time of deep need. He risked his own reputation and standing in the kingdom and even his place as the next person in line to the throne; his father could easily have disowned him for being David's closest friend.

First Samuel 23:16 says, "And Saul's son Jonathan went to David at Horesh and helped him find strength in God." It touches me that Jonathan didn't wait for David to find his way back home—he went looking for him. Jonathan wanted to offer spiritual comfort and encouragement to David, not through words given to a messenger to deliver but through his physical presence—his nearness to David in his time of need. And when he found him, Jonathan poured strength and life back into David. That's sustaining friendship.

You've probably heard some variation of the following quotation attributed to Elbert Hubbard: "In order to have a friend you must first be a friend." I know that good friendships are built on mutuality, but there have been many times in my life when I couldn't summon up the strength to do the work of maintaining a friendship. Depression or illness or exhaustion or grief had taken too high of a toll. Some of my sustaining friends came looking for me when I couldn't go looking for them. When they found me, they poured strength and life back into me, encouraging me to keep trusting God no matter what. Their love allowed me to keep walking on my journey.

When you're a pastor's wife, how do you find friends like these? Most of the time we become friends with someone accidentally—it just happens as our lives intersect on a regular basis and we discover common interests. Some of my dearest friendships developed as we worked side by side on a ministry project or ended up in a women's Bible study together. But there's also a time to intentionally seek to build a close friendship. Here are my suggestions to consider:

- Look for spiritually mature women. A new Christian probably can't handle the fact that you have "stuff."
- Start casually, sharing small bits of personal information to see if this person remains confidential. There's nothing worse than having private information you shared in confidence suddenly become common knowledge.
- Look for women who don't "need" you. Women who need to share your spotlight, bask in your perks, or enjoy the importance of being your friend will not be there when things get tough. When our church was very small, my closest friend never sought to sit by me or even talk to me at an event. She was content to wave at me from across the room, knowing that later that day we'd call each other and talk at leisure. She definitely didn't need my attention in public to validate the friendship.

- A personal crisis will clear the decks of all but your closest friends, and while it's painful to realize that some of the people you assumed would be there for you in a time of need didn't show up, you'll be touched by the people who did. Hold on to them.

- Remember that some friendships have seasons. Circumstances change, and so do people. Learn to be grateful for the gifts of love and care a friend brought you in a particular season without demanding everything remain the same. Know that God will bring another friend in his time. Keep your heart open.

Even if you follow these practical guidelines for building healthy friendships, you need to accept the reality that a friend may unexpectedly wound you deeply. She could betray your confidence, gossip about you, take sides against you, treat you with disrespect, or quietly undermine you and then deny it to your face. I can't say it won't happen, but the benefits of intimacy are worth the risks of hurt.

One last thought. When talking to some of the other pastors' wives at Saddleback, they asked, "Is it ever okay to say I can't handle any more relationships?" Oh yes! It is completely okay to draw lines and boundaries around yourself. You don't have an infinite capacity for relationships. When you're juggling kids and all that entails, the maintenance of your home, perhaps a job, keeping the connection between you and your husband strong and vibrant, nurturing your alone time with Jesus, and ministering to hurting women in the church, you may not have time for lunch with the girls. It's okay to say no to one more offer of friendship. Handle it with as much kindness as possible. I say things like, "That is so kind of you; I wish I could join you at _____, but I won't be able to do it. It means the world to me that you would ask." As a people pleaser, this has been a challenging skill for me to develop. I don't want to disappoint anyone. But I have learned to say no with a smile, and I don't feel the need to justify my reasons. I can read the sadness on the faces of some people—and I hate it—but I am merely human. My emotional and physical resources—and yours—are not limitless. We need to recognize the necessity of safeguarding our energy to prevent burnout.

The Beauty of a Shared Life

My prayer for you is that you will push back against the instinct for self-protection that creates isolation and loneliness.

- Remember that we are merely human beings. We cannot walk on water, live on top of a teetering pedestal, or exist inside the constrictive box of perfectionism.
- Make the decision to get down off the pedestal—today—and refuse to climb back up on it.
- Be careful not to perpetuate your ideal self with your congregation but your real self.
- Embrace God's view of you—dearly loved, accepted, and graced.
- Walk in the light of God's grace so the dark things in your soul will find healing as they are exposed to the light.
- Seek a shared life with other flawed human beings who are also walking in the light, allowing yourself to deeply know and to be known.

- Determine to be the kind of friend who helps others find strength in God.

It's humbling to acknowledge your humanity and to refuse to allow church members to elevate you to a higher status than you can live up to. It's difficult to keep walking in the light when every fiber of your being tells you to run back to the safety of the shadows. It's risky to deliberately reveal your real self as you seek satisfying relationships. But as with David and Jonathan, it is in true friendship that our souls find strength in God. We were made to share life together.

Taking Care of Yourself

When the heart is right, the mind
and the body will follow.

CORETTA SCOTT KING,
wife of Martin Luther King Jr.

When we consider moving to a new job, one of the most important questions we ask is, "What are the benefits like?" We want to know about health insurance, retirement plans, vacation days, sick days, and paid and unpaid leave. In essence, we're asking, "Are you going to take care of me?" That's a great question. In many ways, this is the unspoken question we ask in all of our relationships: "Are you going to take care of me? Will you meet my needs?" But if you expect a church or a husband or a friend to take care of you, you're in for a real disappointment.

The truth is no one will take care of you but you.

That might sound cynical, but it reflects reality. I'm not putting down the people in your life and implying they don't love you well. I'm just pointing out your personal obligation to look out for yourself—to own your responsibility for self-care.

Song of Solomon 1:6 says, "I had no time to care for myself" (GNT). These words are attributed to the Shulammite woman who lamented her work in someone else's vineyard that kept her from caring for the things that mattered to her. Every woman could say these words at some point—"I had no time to care for myself"—but especially pastors' wives who find themselves so immersed in ministry, job, and family concerns that there is simply no time to nurture their personal well-being. But years of neglect can yield consequences none of us want: burnout; poor physical, emotional, and spiritual health; and loneliness. I want to suggest four intentional ways we should seek to be as whole and healthy for life and ministry as we can be.

⸺ Eat, Sleep, Move ⸺

Rick is the master of one-liners, and he's famous for them around here. Staff members quiz one another on his more memorable ones, seeing who can remember the most. Our kids tease him mercilessly, using his sermon lines to get his goat.

My collection of one-liners is much smaller, but I hope I'm remembered for this one: control the controllables and leave the uncontrollables to God. Because I am prone to anxiety and am therefore a bit of a control freak, this is a lesson I learn again each new sunrise. We all know the impossibility of controlling every element of our fragile lives, yet many of us yield too much ground to what is impossible and ignore what is possible.

Much is within our control if we choose to take charge. It's far easier, however, to blame somebody else for our dissatisfaction or unhappiness. "If my husband/kids/church were different, I'd be different." Maybe it's time to hold up the mirror and take a good, honest look at the real source of many of your struggles: you.

Control the controllables and *leave* the uncontrollables to God.

For decades, I denied this principle when it came to my physical health—specifically, what I eat, how much I sleep, and how much I move. I'm not an athlete. I hate to sweat. Seriously. I hate it. But I also injured my lower back as a teenager and spent the next twenty years fighting major back problems, culminating in two surgeries to repair what was damaged. I got used to being ultraprotective of my bad back, and exercise always seemed to cause more pain.

And I love to bake. Notice I didn't say I love to cook. I love to *bake*. The sweeter, chocolate-ier, and more decadent the better. Cakes, cookies, pies, candies, frostings, fillings, toppings, desserts of every type—yum! I guess I can sum it up by saying I *love* sugar. When I half-heartedly sought help with my health a few years back, the physician suggested I replace sugar with stevia, a plant-based natural sweetener. I looked him right in the eye and heatedly announced, "I would rather get Alzheimer's disease than give up sugar."

Being the competent, unflappable physician he is, he didn't fall out of his chair in shock or get all bent out of shape. He calmly looked me right back in the eye and said, "Is that true?"

"Yes," I said. "Absolutely."

He replied with understatement, "That's a pretty strong attachment to sugar." I think I blocked out the rest of the conversation because that was undoubtedly one of the stupidest things I had ever said. But at that moment I had no intention of addressing my love of sugar.

To make my approach to my health at that time even more disastrous, I was having a hard time sleeping because Matthew was doing poorly; his suicidal thoughts and attempts were wearing me down. Nights were the worst; I slept with my phone nearby because that was usually when his dark depression took its toll. I got used to waking up to the slightest vibration of my cell phone, and our middle-of-the-night texting conversations sometimes lasted hours. Even on the nights we weren't texting or talking, I could never seem to turn off the drumbeat of anguish and anxiety I felt over my precious boy. I don't think I slept through an entire night for years.

There were circumstances out of my control. I couldn't control my bad back. I couldn't control Matthew or the havoc mental illness was causing in his life and in our lives. I couldn't heal him or make him "normal"; I couldn't even comfort him sometimes. I let what I couldn't control start to control what I *could* control. And that doesn't even take into account the things I could control and just didn't want to.

I got serious about taking care of myself because I want to last in life and in ministry. I asked myself what it would look like if I took Romans 12:1 seriously and really offered my body to God as a living sacrifice. What would I do differently? What would it take to make my body stronger and healthier so that I could increase my physical capacity to serve the Lord?

I started paying attention to what I eat—how much, what quality, and what type. I'm not rigid in my eating habits, but I am aware that food can be a powerful ally in staying healthy or a powerful enemy of good health. I started walking regularly and doing Pilates twice a week, along with some exercises based on biomechanics. I stopped staying up as late and tried to gently wind down at the end of the day rather than working on my unfinished to-do list until all hours of the night. This new routine has been especially necessary as my body, mind, and soul process Matthew's death; taking care of *me* is an essential part of moving through grief.

What does this have to do with you? What does this have to do with a life in ministry?

Your story may have similarities to mine—or be completely different. What is the same is our ability to exert control over much more of our health than we are usually willing to acknowledge. You control what food you put in your mouth—the quality and the quantity. You control whether you move your body in some form of exercise or not. You control whether you stay up until midnight watching Netflix or go to bed at 10:30 p.m. This is what it means to control the controllables.

I'm assuming you want to last in the ministry. I'm hoping you want to be as strong, vibrant, and vital spiritually, emotionally, physically, and mentally as you possibly can for as long as you can. I'm hoping you truly desire in your soul to honor God with the body he has entrusted into your care. Good! And to make those goals come true, you will need to do something different than what you're doing now. You will need to eat well, sleep well, and move well.

I'm not a nutritionist or a dietician or an expert on health. What I know is that I am almost 100 percent in charge of my health—and you are too. We may not be able to control every element of our health—I'm not saying that—but to the degree that we can, we must. Our bodies are containers of the Holy Spirit of God—they hold the sacred in fragile jars of clay. We regularly abuse these jars of clay and then wonder why we can't serve the Lord more fully. I want to last; I want to serve God with all that I have. I don't want to get sick because I was careless with what God entrusted into my hands. I might have a stroke or a heart attack or endure another bout with cancer someday, but it won't be because I didn't control the controllables. It won't be because I acted thoughtlessly and squandered a healthy body. I can't control the uncontrollables—they're in God's hands—but I'm responsible for what is in *my* hands.

So today think about what you're eating. Think about how you could add movement to your daily life. Think about your bedtime routine. Your life and ministry may just depend on these things.

⸺ Nourish Your Inner Life ⸺

From what I've observed, the secret to resilience—the ability to survive tough and challenging life circumstances—is not intelligence, gifting, or even anointing. Resilience starts with a *decision* to take care of yourself in a holistic way—to nurture yourself physically, emotionally, and spiritually. Those who bounce back more readily from pain and loss have taken self-care seriously, with a particular focus on the inner life.

Gail MacDonald, in her classic book on ministry, *High Call, High Privilege*, tells of hearing a retired missionary compare our passion and zeal for Christ to a fire burning in our hearts that must be managed lest the flames go out. "Untended fires soon die and become a pile of ashes," he said. This gentleman went on to urge his listeners to give serious attention to the condition of the internal fire, noting that if we don't pay attention, "all attempts at finding one's way through the challenges of life will be relatively futile."[1]

This story—which I first read in 1981—has stayed with me. It has caused me to continually evaluate the state of my own inner fire, to look for ways I am allowing the bright, warm flames to diminish into embers that are on the verge of being extinguished. When that little fire of who we are begins to die due to busyness, neglect, or painful circumstances, we have nothing to give to the people in our lives. I don't know about you, but I have experienced the emptiness of trying to minister from a stone-cold heart. It is unsettling to realize you don't care about the needs of your family, friends, neighbors, or congregation—not because you're a bad person but because somehow you've neglected to maintain and guard the inner fire and not one ember is still burning.

Resilience starts with a *decision* to take care of yourself in a *holistic* way— to nurture yourself physically, emotionally, and spiritually.

We all face stresses and pressures that threaten to take us out, stresses and pressures that pull us away from tending the fires of passion and zest for living, stresses and pressures that make us think we're one conversation away from exploding into a billion bits. You might experience it as an overwhelming desire to run, to escape, to just leave it all. If your heart is cold or barren or you're resisting the urge to get out now, pay attention. Please.

Charles Swindoll tells of visiting the home of a wealthy couple and noticing words carved on an intricate, wooden mantel. He stepped closer and read: "If your heart is cold my fire cannot warm it."[2]

What a powerful reminder that temporary pleasures cannot warm a cold heart—not a beautiful fireplace or a new dress or a drink or a vacation or an affair. We try all the wrong ways to restart the fire that has dwindled within us. None of those things will warm our hearts when they're cold. Swindoll says the only way to warm a cold heart is to turn back to intimacy with our God, who is referred to eleven times in the Bible as the "consuming fire." He alone can restart the inner fire.

No one but you is responsible for your spiritual life. No one can force you to grow in your faith. Your husband is not going to stand over you every morning and insist that you have a quiet time with the Lord. He can't memorize Scripture for you. He can't give you a heart of surrender. No one but you can grow a deep soul inside of you. It's up to you to share the life of the vine and abide in Christ. John 15:4–5 says, "You must go on growing in me and I will grow in you. For just as the branch cannot bear any fruit unless it shares the life of the vine, so you can produce nothing unless you go on growing in me. I am the vine itself, you are the branches. It is the man who shares my life and whose life I share who proves fruitful. For the plain fact is that apart from me you can do nothing at all" (Phillips).

My daughter, Amy, who is a pastor's wife, has chronic Lyme disease and has been ill for almost half of her life. As you might imagine, there have been dramatic swings between better health and relapses. Some days she blows me away with what she can accomplish, but other days just brushing her teeth counts as a successful day. She has learned the hard way that her only hope of riding the waves of chronic illness is to abide in Jesus, to daily seek intimacy with him. Otherwise, the task of raising three small children, ministering to hurting neighbors and friends, and supporting her husband in ministry is simply beyond her capacity.

She says, "Christianity is an inside job, which means my internal reality has the power to rise up and overwhelm my external circumstances if I choose to learn God's ways. As the painful circumstances have piled up over the years, I have had to choose to go underground (so to speak) spiritually to survive. The above-ground reality has been so painful, terrifying, and seemingly hopeless that withdrawing inward to a soul space with God has been necessary. But there, in what one would assume would be darkness, I have found light. I have found Jesus ready to empower and comfort me, to share his peace and give me his joy. With more physical healing under my belt, the challenge is to stay in this place of intimacy with Jesus, to not just visit occasionally but to actually live out of this internal reality. Abiding has become the single-minded daily pursuit of my soul."

Some of you have paid attention to your body, your mind, and your soul; you're abiding as closely with Jesus as you know how; you've done everything you can think of to feel better, but you don't. It's entirely possible that you're experiencing depression. If so, you're not alone, dear sister. Please don't feel even one second of shame or embarrassment. Biblical figures, early church fathers and mothers, respected theologians, and famous pastors and church leaders throughout the centuries—as well as many of the readers of this book—have lived or are living with bouts of depression. It's not a sin to be depressed. You're not weak or flawed, and you don't have a character defect. You're not a spiritual baby. Depression is an illness; it's real, it's common, and it's treatable. It's vital that you understand that untreated depression can be lethal. Make an appointment to see your primary care physician as soon as possible and talk to her about your symptoms. She may run some lab tests to check a variety of conditions that could be affecting your mood, and she may recommend you see a psychiatrist for a more thorough evaluation. She may suggest you take a medication to help manage the bleak darkness that depression can bring. No matter what, don't be afraid to have a conversation with your doctor and don't wait!

Of course, it's such a comfort to also be able to discuss how you're feeling with a trusted friend or small group member and to find a listening ear, encouragement, and prayer. We're whole beings—body, mind, and soul—so attack depression on every level possible. Take care of yourself physically, emotionally, and relationally. Most of all, don't suffer alone in silence; don't hide your pain from your brothers and sisters in Christ. As we've already said, you're a part of the body of Christ, and when one member hurts, we all hurt. As Larry Crabb insists, the church must be the safest place on earth, where we can bring our broken selves, our depressed selves, our addicted selves, our anxious selves—all of who we are and who we are not—and find not only a welcome embrace but also fellow strugglers who will journey with us no matter how long it takes.

—— Observe a Sabbath ——

I can't talk about taking care of yourself without talking about taking days off, vacations, and observing a Sabbath—finding ways to disconnect from ministry responsibilities weekly. I realize I'm probably preaching to the choir because it's almost always our husbands who are lax in taking an adequate amount of time off, right? In fact, in the survey I took, more than half of the women who responded said that their husbands do not take adequate time off. Many said either the church doesn't offer as much time off as they feel is necessary or their husbands struggle to let go of responsibilities and really rest.

Eugene Peterson, one of the most respected theologians of our day, says:

> One of the hard things in America is to escape this scheduled world that we're living in—where things are so disconnected from the seasons, from the night and day, the rhythms that are around us and that are within us, our heartbeat, our pulse, our breathing. So if we just let the culture determine the way we live, we're going to live pretty jerky lives. I think for me, and for many I've worked with and talked to around this, the place to begin is the Sabbath. The Sabbath is the one interruption into the life of jerky fragmentation that is still possible. You can take a day off.[3]

We know it's biblical—the Ten Commandments are pretty clear about a weekly Sabbath—so why is it so hard to implement? There are several reasons, but two oft-recurring reasons are:

1. The walk-on-water syndrome. We think the church *needs* us and can't function without our attention 24/7. One of the many results of this unhealthy syndrome is a codependent congregation and pastor. The more we remain available at all times, the more church members will stay helpless, locking us into an ongoing dysfunctional relationship.

2. A misunderstanding of the theology of the body of Christ. We've talked about how the church is the body of Christ and has a variety of parts that should work together for the good of the whole. If your husband does not equip the other parts of the body to do the work of ministry, their gifts will go unused, robbing them of the joy and fulfillment of serving and preventing him from getting the rest and renewal he needs to stay healthy.

I watched these two misunderstandings play out in the churches I grew up in. There wasn't an emphasis on equipping the saints for the work of the ministry. In the minds of the parishioners, the *minister* was supposed to do the ministry. My dad was the paid professional, and he was expected to make every hospital visit, visit every shut-in, visit prospective and lapsed members, conduct every wedding and funeral, teach or preach at multiple events every week, *plus* attend numerous committee and board meetings—no matter how depleted or weary he was. This is just wrong! If your husband is on this hamster wheel of busyness, point him to Ephesians 4:12–13 and remind him that the congregation is made up of *ministers* who have been gifted so they can *minister*.

Let's be honest about another potential roadblock to a day off and vacations that isn't theological but very real. If your husband isn't the senior pastor, he probably doesn't have as much say over how much time he is allowed to take off, or even if time off is allowed on paper, in the day-to-day real world of deadlines and unexpected meetings, he might feel pressured to put in extra hours. This situation pits a husband against his frustrated family or against his senior pastor or leadership team, a no-win situation for sure.

While the first two reasons we don't take time off are easier to resolve than this one (because they're theological and should be addressed on that level), there is no one solution when you are not the senior pastor and are at the mercy of those who serve over you. Each situation is different and the way you approach the people holding the vacation purse strings is individual, but I truly believe your first responsibility is to your husband's ability to last over the long haul as well as to your family's health and well-being. If you need to change churches, change churches. As much as is possible and within your control, plant your family in a church with like-minded values about long-term spiritual, emotional, and physical health.

—— Create a Rejuvenating Routine ——

Growing up in a conservative, evangelical home, our rituals concerning the Sabbath were pretty simple—and they were mostly a lot of don'ts. Don't go shopping, don't go to a restaurant, don't go to a movie, and don't play cards. Sunday certainly wasn't a day of rest for our family unless you count the afternoon nap in between Sunday school/Sunday morning worship and Sunday evening services.

No, we were Monday people. I grew up thinking everybody's daddy took Mondays off. They were simple times. We parked our car at the outdoor mall and watched people walk by. I'm not kidding. We got a small burger and fries from Jack in the Box and a small orange freeze from Dairy Queen, and we were set for hours of fun musings about the people we observed. That's what you do when you don't have money to spend at the mall.

There were lots of picnics and camping adventures as well, but Mondays were meant for people watching.

Rick and I continued the Monday-off tradition after we started Saddleback. He has often said he hates to feel that bad on his day off, but after preaching up to six services each weekend, he's limp spaghetti by Monday morning and desperately in need of some downtime. Rick is a self-admitted workaholic, and to be completely transparent, I can give him a run for his money sometimes when it comes to overworking. That didn't used to be true, but once I started working full-time after our kids left home, I changed. I can get just as caught up in deadlines to meet, projects that need my attention, and messages to prepare as he can. That's one of the reasons we have always taken a day off each week—always. It's also the reason we take the same day off every week unless there's a compelling reason to change it. We've found that if we intend to take a day off at some point in the week but don't keep it as a regularly scheduled day, there will always be some important meeting or appointment or task that pushes the day off into the next week . . . or the week after that . . . or the week after that. So Mondays it is.

When the kids were small, we traded babysitting with neighbors so we had a few blissful hours to ourselves. After the kids got older and were in school, Monday night was family night— a sacred time that was almost inviolable. The kids took turns choosing where we ate dinner and what we did, ranging from hotdogs at Weinerschnitzel and testing new video games at Best Buy to hamburgers in the backyard and board games and everything in between. Family night never cost a lot of money; the value was time spent together.

These days Rick is close to heaven when he's digging in his garden, lovingly tending his plants or vegetables, letting his mind find rest in quiet communion with Jesus—and no talking! Give the guy some fresh dirt, a shovel, and some seeds and he is oblivious to the rest of the world. A hike, a shower later in the day, something yummy to eat, alone time with me, and he's ready to hit the ground again on Tuesday.

Because we have Saturday night services, I've started attending one of them with my kids and grandkids, allowing me for the first time in my entire life to be home on Sunday mornings. Can I tell you that it is pure, unadulterated bliss? It's the only time in the week I'm there alone, and I jealously hoard each minute. I've created rituals that make the brief hours rich with meaning and renewal. I even have a special mug I drink my tea from. It says, "Easy Like Sunday Morning." It's a bit tongue-in-cheek—Sunday mornings *easy*? I won't let myself drink from it any other day—it's reserved for my Sabbath time on Sundays. Now before you hate me for having Sunday mornings to myself, I'm keenly aware that life and circumstances could go through another huge change at any moment and I'll be seeing quiet Sunday mornings in my rearview mirror.

I walk outside when the weather cooperates (which is pretty often) and watch the birds fight over space on a tree branch. I close my eyes and try to pick up smells and sounds that I might overlook if my eyes were open. I sit in silence, noting the whispers of God's presence all around me. I often sit at my piano and play through the hymnal—I mean I start with page 1 and get through at least a third to a half of the hymnal. I play until my fingers and wrists ache and my voice is raspy—or until I've cried enough. Sometimes the tears flow because a memory is attached to a hymn; sometimes I cry because the lyrics speak so powerfully of the hope of heaven; sometimes I am just overwhelmed by who God is and amazed that he loves me. Then I start putzing around the house—leisurely doing a load of laundry, randomly straightening out-of-place items, or pulling out a fun, new recipe I've been wanting to try—but all at a gentle, unhurried pace that allows for meditation and reflection. Within a few hours, I am renewed, ready to reengage with my family, my friends, and the world.

Do you have rituals that make your Sabbath holy, set apart, disconnected from the church; routines that create distance from normal life and responsibilities; chances to be quiet and still; moments to do the things that pour life back into you? Jesus calls us to rest in Mark 6:31: "Then, because so many people were coming and going that they did not even have a chance to eat, he said to them, 'Come with me by yourselves to a quiet place and get some rest.'"

Can you hear Jesus's invitation here? Rather than berate the disciples for not getting more done—for not organizing another event for the crowds—he recognizes their weariness and their need to be alone with him in a quiet place so they can rest. Whether you've let your inner fire go out due to disobedience or it's been smothered by grief, poor health, or overcommitment, his offer is the same: Come be with me. By yourself. Without the noise and chaos of everyday life. Please rest.

Peter Scazzero, author of *Emotionally Healthy Spirituality*, says, "We imitate God by stopping our work and resting."[4] I could be wrong on what I'm about to say, but I don't think so. Taking a day off and filling it with activity is against the spirit of Sabbath, which is about quietness and rest from activity. I realize

I'm more of a be-er than a do-er, and those with a more energetic personality might argue that they connect more readily with God while they're doing something. There's nothing wrong with doing fun activities on your day off, but I have a hard time believing that only cleaning out the garage or going to a movie with friends is what a Sabbath is about. *Somewhere* in the twenty-four hours of Sabbath, activity, noise, productivity, and interaction must cease—including all electronic devices. This takes some getting used to for those of us who cannot breathe without our cell phones, but even if just for fifteen minutes, be quiet, disconnect, and rest.

> *Somewhere* in the twenty-four hours of *Sabbath,* activity, noise, productivity, and interaction must *cease*—including all electronic devices.

Be Well

Years ago Rick bought a used car with very few miles on it from a little old lady in Leisure World. We took it to Tijuana for a cheap paint job and new leather seats. Hence its affectionate name, La Bamba. One day we noticed that a balloon had developed on the edge of the driver's side front tire—it was bulging and ready to explode. With great fear and trepidation, Rick and a friend—who called the damaged tire a "widow maker"—carefully changed it, knowing that if it exploded while they were working on it, disaster could happen.

Don't let life and ministry take you to the place of blowing up . . . or walking away . . . or going numb . . . or giving up. Please take good care of yourself. Take charge of the controllables and leave the uncontrollables to God. Pay attention to your body and honor it as God's dwelling place. Pay attention to your soul; fan the flames of passion for Jesus so the warm fire of intimacy keeps burning brightly year after year. Monitor your emotional life; make sure you create space for the activities that pour life back into you. Pay attention to your mind and emotions, and seek help if depression or anxiety settles in. Boldly seek uninterrupted time for you and your husband and with your children so you can be replenished and restored. Remember the Sabbath day by keeping it holy. Be well, my sisters.

Valuing Seasons and Moments

Whatever the particular call is, the particular sacrifice God asks you to make, the particular cross He wishes you to embrace, whatever the particular path He wants you to tread, will you rise up, and say in your heart, "Yes, Lord, I accept it; I submit, I yield, I pledge myself to walk in that path, and to follow that Voice, and to trust Thee with the consequences"? Oh! but you say, "I don't know what He will want next." No, we none of us know that, but we know we shall be safe in His hands.

CATHERINE BOOTH,
wife of William Booth

E cclesiastes 3:1–8 teaches that God balances the natural world through seasons, and each season has a function and a purpose in God's overall design of the earth's fragile ecosystems and even more fragile inhabitants. These verses confirm that life comes to us in small segments.

> There is a time for everything,
>> and a season for every activity under the heavens:
>> a time to be born and a time to die,
>> a time to plant and a time to uproot,
>> a time to kill and a time to heal,
>> a time to tear down and a time to build,
>> a time to weep and a time to laugh,
>> a time to mourn and a time to dance,
>> a time to scatter stones and a time to gather them,
>> a time to embrace and a time to refrain from
>>> embracing,
>> a time to search and a time to give up,
>> a time to keep and a time to throw away,
>> a time to tear and a time to mend,
>> a time to be silent and a time to speak,
>> a time to love and a time to hate,
>> a time for war and a time for peace.

Day in, day out. There is a time for children to be conceived in the darkness of the womb and a time for all of us to return to the dust from which we came. There is a time for seeds to lie dormant in the ground and a time for them to explode with visible, above-ground growth. Day in, day out. A time for everything and a season for every activity under heaven. The rhythm of nature is repeated endlessly season after season.

I believe that life and ministry also come to us in seasons. But the seasons of life and ministry, unlike those of nature, are not determined by the predictable phases of the moon or the expected growth cycle of a seed. Life and ministry are more complicated and far less precise, and a single event can catapult us from one season to another in a heartbeat. The uncertainty, unpredictability, and rapid change often create stress—sometimes intense stress that can lead to one of the reasons pastors leave the ministry: burnout. How can we experience peace and rest for our souls in the changing seasons of life and ministry? Here's what I know: learn the unforced rhythms of grace, commit your daily schedule to God, adjust for the season you're in, and enjoy the moments.

Learn the Unforced Rhythms of Grace

Matthew 6:33 says, "Seek the Kingdom of God above all else, and live righteously, and he will give you everything you need" (NLT). Or as the King James Version says, "Seek ye first the kingdom of God."

This verse has always created anxiety for me. Even as a child I felt enormous pressure to get this right. It has always been my desire to seek first the kingdom of God in everything I do.

The tricky part is figuring out *how* to make sure I'm seeking God and his kingdom first in my life. I'm a rule-following perfectionist who takes things literally, so I was on a search for the surefire, guaranteed litmus test to ascertain whether Jesus was at the center. I like things to be black and white, so when people I respected suggested living by a list of priorities, I happily adopted that approach. I mean, who doesn't like to check off the boxes? Most of you would probably agree with the list of priorities I was given: God first. Check. Husband second. Check. Kids third. Check. From there it gets a little murky, but my list said church and ministry fourth, so check.

Work next? Check. Friends next? Check. All the other people and needs of the world? Check. Check. The list was supposed to give me clear guidelines for making sure I was putting God first, and I tried. I really, really tried—hard—but over time my anxiety only increased.

Here was my dilemma. If I woke up in the morning and my first thought was of Rick instead of God, was I putting Rick first? If my kids and their needs came first to mind, was I putting them before God? If so, I was doomed to failure day after day because I just couldn't make that priority list cooperate with the realities of my life.

When we try to live by a list of priorities, we are inviting complete frustration because it's an impossible way to live. I don't believe that's what God means when he says to seek first his kingdom. I've begun to think instead of a wheel with spokes attached to the hub. I'm the wheel, Jesus is the hub, and every relationship and responsibility I have are the spokes. A wheel falls apart—it won't even function—if the spokes aren't attached to the hub. Christ is at the center of our lives, and we fall apart and can't function if we are not connected to him. Everything I do comes out of my relationship to him. He's not off to the side of the wheel, nor is he one of many spokes in the wheel. He's in the center, keeping every part of my life working as it should. When I'm connected to Jesus, it affects the kind of wife I am, the kind of mother I am, the kind of minister I am, the kind of friend I am. As life circumstances morph and change each day, I can rest easier because I know I'm walking in tandem with him.

Another oft-repeated concept is that we should seek balanced lives, with each domain of our lives receiving an equal amount of time and attention. It sounds so reasonable and looks so logical on paper. Like living by a list of priorities, though, this approach usually only leads to more frustration.

Eugene Peterson suggests that rhythm replace our quest for balance and living by a list of priorities. His paraphrase of Matthew 11:28–30 is richly layered poetry:

> Are you tired? Worn out? Burned out on religion? Come to me. Get away with me and you'll recover your life. I'll show you how to take a real rest. Walk with me and work with me—watch how I do it. Learn the unforced rhythms of grace. I won't lay anything heavy or ill-fitting on you. Keep company with me and you'll learn to live freely and lightly. (Message)

In an interview with Gabe Lyons, Peterson explains what he means by a life in rhythm:

> Let me qualify this by saying that rhythm is very individual. You can't impose a rhythm on somebody; you have to enter into a rhythm. And people don't have to have the same rhythm. Some people can walk in three-quarter time and some in four-four time. You don't have to do it the same. You can't do it the same. You've got to find the rhythm of your own body, your own life, your own history. Having rhythm means that you live out who you are in relationship to who God is, who Jesus is. So it's more like a dance.[1]

Another word picture that might help us think about seeking God first while living with flesh-and-blood people who have needs is that of a river. We start with the full awareness that God is our dearest desire and that "in him we live and move and have our being" (Acts 17:28). He is with us every moment—never leaving us for one second of our earthly existence. And with us in him and he in us, we step into the "river" of daily life. A river does not flow at exactly the same pace every day. It is affected by circumstances: weather conditions or whether somebody came in and dammed up a part of it and now the river flows differently. That pretty accurately reflects the fact that things come into our lives every day that change the ebb and flow of our lives and where we're putting our time and attention. Instead of living by a list of priorities, we fluidly ebb and flow with the changing needs of our husbands, children, work, and ministries as the days of our lives go by.

Because we know there is an ebb and flow to our existence, we don't become overly stressed out by the heavier flow of the river on a particular day—it's temporary. We give time and attention here, and then the river shifts and we give time and attention there. We learn how to commit our daily schedules to God.

—— Commit Your Daily Schedule to God ——

I don't know how many of you are to-do list makers, but I am a compulsive list maker. I've got them everywhere—on scraps of paper, on big pieces of paper, on my computer. I've even been known to scribble them on my hand. I blame my mother.

What I have discovered is that life never cooperates with my to-do lists. Ever. Have any of you experienced that? You've got your day planned. You know what's supposed to happen. You know who you're supposed to talk to, you know who you're supposed to see, you know what tasks you're supposed to accomplish. You've got it all set out. Then life and interruptions come and what you had planned to do just doesn't get done, just doesn't happen the way you think it should. I can get really upset about that.

When my kids were at home, I used to tell them, "Woe to the child who messes with Mama's schedule. You are asking for serious trouble." I've since learned it is a sign of immaturity to get uptight when your schedule doesn't go the way you want it to go. On the reverse, it is a sign of growing godliness when you are flexible and bendable as life comes your way.

When we put Psalm 31:15, "My times are in your hands," into practice, we reduce the stress in our lives. This verse becomes a prayer. "My times are in your hands, God. You are directing my life. You know the things I'm supposed to get done." So if interruptions come, if things go differently, I can either get all bent out of shape and angry at the people who interrupted me or the situations that messed up my schedule, or I can flow with the changes in a gracious way, believing that God has my times in his hands.

Mark 5:21–43 begins with Jesus on his way to heal the dying daughter of Jairus, a synagogue leader. It's an emergency situation. As Jesus heads to Jairus's house to heal the dying child, a woman with a chronic health problem—the Bible says she has been bleeding continuously for twelve years—approaches Jesus to touch his clothes. She believes if she does so, she'll be healed. She touches the hem of his robe, and he instantly knows and turns to speak to her. Anyone in an emergency situation knows you don't stop for nonemergencies—you put all of your energy into taking care of the life-and-death situation first. We call that triage. But in an astonishing response to the woman with a non-life-and-death condition, he pauses, talks to her, and heals her.

That just doesn't compute to me. Here is a girl who is near death. In fact, while Jesus lingers with the woman, Jairus receives word that his daughter has died. Shouldn't Jesus get it in gear and madly rush to revive her? Instead, he stops and talks to a woman who isn't dying, who isn't in an emergency, who isn't in a critical situation. You have to ask the question, Why did he do that? Why did he allow someone to interrupt him and even detain him in the middle of a very serious situation?

Scripture is never random or meaningless, so there must be deep truth hidden in this odd, seemingly illogical, if not unkind (to Jairus and his daughter) encounter. I wonder if the principle we should grasp is this: sometimes the interrupted is not as important as the interrupter. Did you get that? We often act as though our plans for the day, our agendas, are sacred—untouchable and completely uninterruptable. But God might know something we don't and allow us to be interrupted, which often completely destroys our carefully constructed to-do lists. Evidently, there are times when the interrupter—a child, a friend, a stranger, a situation—is more important than the interrupted—me.

Honestly, I don't like that. I still want my schedule. But the truth is God knows what my day should hold. God knows what your day should hold. He knew before you got up this morning what was going to happen to you today. He knew the emergencies. He knew the things that weren't emergencies but that were going to masquerade as emergencies. He knew the things that were going to come into your life and were going to derail you from what you thought you were supposed to do and who you were supposed to talk to and what you were supposed to accomplish.

I don't have the answer other than to say that too often we assume the interruptions are not important. Too often we think we know what today is supposed to hold and that an interruption can't be as important as what we had set out to do.

What I'm trying to learn to do is to pause and say, "Okay, God, my times are in your hands. You knew what this day was going to hold before I did, so this interruption—child, husband, phone call, unexpected demand on my time—is in your hands. Don't let me make the arrogant mistake of assuming that my schedule is what must be honored, not the interruption that you bring."

Don't mishear me. Every interruption that comes your way is not important. Sometimes interruptions come because we live in a broken world and bad things happen. A three-car pileup on the road in front of you isn't necessarily a good interruption. But with every interruption we have the opportunity to go to God, to seek his face, to talk to him, and to hear his voice. He'll either let you know that the interruption is part of what he has for you today or give you the insight to be able to sidestep the interruption so you can get back to the task or goal at hand. In either case, he'll give you the grace to know that everything is in his control no matter what.

Adjust for the Season You're In

It seems that American women have bought into the fantasy that they can do it all, have it all, and be it all—all at the same time. You can have a fabulous relationship with God. You can have a fabulous marriage. You can have a fabulous family. You can have a fabulous career. You can have a fabulous ministry. And you can have it all while wearing fabulous shoes!

I can count on one hand the number of women I have met in my lifetime who were fabulous in every one of those areas at the same time. It's a ridiculously impossible goal we have set for ourselves, and it creates enormous guilt and dissatisfaction when we fall short of fabulous in any one—or more—of those areas. On top of that, I'm not sure I believe the handful of women who appear to have it all. In my experience, something or someone in our lives pays a steep price for our attempts to have it all at the same time. Something—or someone—is sacrificed along the way. In light of this, Ephesians 5:15–16 is vital instruction: "Be very careful, then, how you live—not as unwise but as wise, making the most of every opportunity, because the days are evil."

At first glance, it might seem as if this verse is urgently calling us to nonstop action and should be accompanied by boldface type, capital letters, and multiple exclamation points: **"Don't miss a single opportunity—EVER—because the universe is winding down. You better get moving NOW if you want to check off all the items on your bucket list for yourself and your family!!"**

This is not the way a wise woman approaches her life—pushing herself and her family to the point of exhaustion; blowing past every boundary of energy, time, and strength; always in a mad rush to get more done and more accomplished on her way to having it all. This is actually the antithesis of these verses.

The Latin origins of the word *circumspectly*, often translated into the English *carefully*, mean "to look around, take heed—be mindful of potential consequences." Other translations use words and phrases such as walk with diligence, caution, accuracy, and exactness; purposefully, worthily, and accurately.

Rather than living life with total spontaneity, with little to no thought about the consequences and ignoring caution, we are to really *look*—live with our eyes wide open—at the true and accurate picture of our circumstances, and from that place of accurate assessment, we are to "redeem the time because the days are evil."

Most commentators agree that the word *redeem* in this passage is not a reference to our salvation (redemption) but a suggestion to "buy back for yourselves." And the Greek word for "time" used here is often translated "opportunity" or "season." So the meaning is to make every opportunity/season your own—to be wise enough to discern when to seize an opportunity and how to use it to the utmost benefit for yourself and for what matters.

The reason we "redeem the time" is because "the days are evil." These are troublesome days—days in which it's more important than ever for a watching world to see believers living sane, thoughtful, and purposeful lives, people who know what matters and aren't caught up in temporary arguments or passing pursuits.

To do otherwise, Scripture says, is to live like a fool—an idiot who is ignorant, witless, spiritually blind, and unaware of what is truly best. The assumption is those who are fools will bypass worthy opportunities; squander precious, irretrievable time; and completely miss moments that cannot be "recalled nor prolonged."[2]

I like the way the Voice translation says it:

So be careful how you live; be mindful of your steps. Don't run around like idiots as the rest of the world does. Instead, walk as the wise! Make the most of every living and breathing moment because these are evil times.

Each season has opportunities that are unique—they are time sensitive and present only in this particular season. With the opportunities there are also limitations—two sides to the same coin. I could tease out the implications of this principle in every domain of your life, but let's take a look at how to make the most of every living and breathing moment as a mother.

Not What You Planned

This is a tender place to begin, but we can't talk about parenting without talking about the season of infertility. Some of you have not been able to have children yet—or maybe that door is firmly closed. There is a tremendous amount of pain in the unfulfilled longing for children. It took years for me to get pregnant with two of my three children, so I can identify in a small way with the aching, waiting, hoping, trying, and tears when the pregnancy test is negative month after endless month. However, I don't know what it's like not to be able to have biological children—to finally stop buying pregnancy tests because there's not going to be a child in my womb. My comments here are spoken with the utmost gentleness and compassion. My sweet sisters, in a season of extreme limitation, there are ultimately a few decisions to be made: focus on the unfulfilled dream in your life or, like many other childless couples, decide to enjoy the opportunity to devote yourselves fully to the Lord in ways you could never do if you had children to care for and raise. The apostle Paul portrays himself in 1 Corinthians 7 as a blessed man with a rich ministry, even though he was single and childless. Other options might include adoption or foster parenting. Perhaps you will conclude that being a physical parent is evidently not in God's plan for you and you will redirect that passion toward being a spiritual "mom" to many others in your extended family, neighborhood, work, or church. The point to remember is this: every season has pain; every season has joy.

Baby, Oh Baby

There is nothing in the world I love more than the smell of a newborn baby's head. If you could bottle it and sell it, I'd buy it by the gallon. I know it sounds weird (and probably is), but I can't help it. I love that musky, earthy smell! Everybody in my church knows to bring me their babies so I can smell their heads—it's like a birthing ritual for new moms. Because the aroma lingers for just a few days before baby shampoo obliterates it, you have to drink it in while it's present. Once it's gone, it's gone.

This is a season with many limitations. There are so many things you simply can't do right now. And that's okay. There are some trade-offs that are infinitely precious; don't rush past them. Enjoy the living and breathing moments with your babies. I promise you the gross diapers, curd-like spit-up, inverted sleeping patterns, screaming for reasons you can't figure out, a carload of paraphernalia just to go to the grocery store, and your constant anxiety that they'll swallow a Lego or a penny will go away. It's also the season of sweet newborn smells, first smiles that melt your heart, tiny trusting hands in yours, and baby arms that encircle your neck. This season will be over before you know it, so don't let the "I can't" moments drown out the "I can" moments.

Time with Toddlers

I remember thinking this season of life would last forever—not in a good way. With toddlers, if you're not digging the newspaper or the cat out of the toilet, you're digging the child out of the toilet. The amount of mayhem and trouble they can get into in the time it takes for you to go to the bathroom will blow your mind. If you've forgotten, start following a young mommy on Instagram and look at her daily feed. You'll crack up at the damage her toddler can create in the space of ten minutes. You know what? The toddler season lasts only a few years. Take advantage of the living and breathing moments to cuddle with that little boy who can still legitimately sit on your lap. Listen to your daughter's silly baby talk. Entertain your son's unanswerable questions—"Why da sky blue, Mommy?"—with patience and good humor. Take advantage of the opportunity to teach some theology to your unsuspecting little one. "I don't know why the sky is blue, sweetheart, but God does. He made the sky!" Yeah, you're exhausted by their antics and boundless energy, but you can sleep in a few years.

Elementary School Years

There's a singular moment in time that spans the toddler years and the elementary school years—the first day of kindergarten. There she is in big-girl clothes, with her little Disney princess lunch box, marching bravely into the school building *without you* for the first time. Rip my heart out and throw it on the ground, why don't you? It got worse. When Matthew started kindergarten, I went home, curled up on the couch, and sobbed. "A season of my life is over. I will never have babies in my home again. I will never have toddlers. I will never send a child off to start kindergarten. I'm so sorry for all the times I griped about the poopy diapers. I'd do it again, God. I would, I really would." I finally managed a prayer of gratitude through my weepy meltdown: "Thank you, God, for the joys; thank you for the trials. Please open another season in front of me—one that is just as precious as this one has been. Give me eyes to see what the next season holds for me."

Clearly, I'm a melancholy and very sentimental. My sister-in-love, Chaundel, held a dance party when her last one went to kindergarten. There were party hats, shouts of jubilation, and noisemakers that could be heard all over her neighborhood. While I sobbed, she giggled and laughed the entire day. Okay, I'm exaggerating, but not everyone gets all teary when a season comes to an end. That's okay too.

To those of you with elementary school children, I just want to say I was lied to. I was told that when my children started school I'd have all these hours of freedom to do what I wanted to do again. They lied. Elementary school means projects your kids neglect to tell you about until two days before the due date, endless hours of homework, after-school sports activities, dance lessons, orthodontist visits, and helping them navigate friendships and the advent of hormones.

You don't have a lot of time to yourself, but you have a few more years of bedtime stories, tucking them in, and marveling as their unique personalities begin to shine. Make the most of these years.

Tumultuous Teens

The teenage years open up a whole new world of limitations and opportunities. Kids get squirrely, do dumb things, make immature choices, and sometimes do things that break our hearts. They grow in their sleep and morph in front of our eyes. Even the cutest little kid has an awkward phase when his face is too big for his body. Her nose is suddenly too big and her teeth need braces badly. They're just odd looking and odd behaving. They and their phone are best friends—inseparable. They also start rewriting history, saying things like, "Remember the time, Mom, when you did such and such?" You say, "No, no, no, that's not the way it happened!" They're absolutely convinced you did this terrible thing to them.

It's so easy to get caught up in the responsibilities of trying to raise decent human beings who stay safe and finish school and keep away from alcohol and drugs. Your focus can be on the hard parts of having teenagers, or you can decide it's a privilege to watch children become men and women before your eyes. You can learn how to gracefully shift from controlling them to coaching them.

Parents in this season find themselves in a constant state of adjustment—nothing stays the same from day to day. But the wise ones start to make the most of the living and breathing moments, to appreciate how precious it is when a little boy who was always so skinny all of a sudden has shoulders out to here, to notice your little girl who's had this pudgy child's body all her life gets breasts and you know she's on her way to being a woman. They don't look like little kids anymore. They're growing up.

Adjust, Adjust, Adjust

So the operative word here is *adjust*. No matter what season of parenting you're in, your life will have limitations. We don't

172

like that. We don't like to be told no. We don't like for anybody to tell us we can't do this or we can't do that or we shouldn't do this or that. But if you understand that each season of life has limitations, you won't push back so hard when you find yourself faced with them. Limitations are not necessarily a bad thing. Limitations are part of the seasons of life that God has given to us.

> *Limitations* are part of the *seasons* of life that God has given to us.

In ministry, the season of life you're in *should* directly have an effect on the level of your involvement. The limitations of babies and toddlers who need a routine, elementary schoolers who need a parent to tuck them in and say prayers with them, and teenagers who are like clams and need you present when they decide to open up and share what's on their hearts should give us boundaries on our service. Maybe it's the time to let a woman in another season of life do the heavy lifting in a particular ministry. You be you and let her be her.

I fit neatly into the demographic of an older Christian woman. My child-rearing days are behind me, and I'm definitely in the latter part of middle age. In this season, I have God-assigned responsibilities to the younger women coming up behind me on the journey. If you're an "older woman," you too are accountable to pass on the wisdom you've accumulated to the next generation of Christian women. One of the limitations in this season is knowing—and accepting—that our children simply don't need us the way they did for decades. Some women don't quite know what to do with themselves and feel a bit lost for a while. Unfortunately, many in this stage breathe a huge sigh of relief thinking their time in the church nursery or as a Sunday school teacher is finally over. Many busy themselves, instead, with all sorts of personal pursuits and projects, often justifying the neglect of their calling to care for the next generation of women by telling themselves that it's finally *my* time.

I once heard Elisabeth Elliot say, "The world is hungry for mothers." I completely agree. *Mothers*, not *Smothers*. Nobody is hungry to be smothered and squelched. But most young women I talk to are desperate to hear from women a few miles farther down the road. There is a loud cry for mentors willing to do life together with single women, married women with no children, women with small children, and women doing their best to figure out their teenagers. Most of us older women underestimate the gift of love and hope we give to a younger woman when we tell her to hold on—that she's going to make it. What life we breathe into a single woman when we applaud the ways she is cultivating her gifts and talents without implying that life begins when she gets a husband. What life we breathe into a young mom when we write a note of encouragement telling her she's going to survive, that she really will not be fishing the cat out of the toilet forever, that she really will not have to be changing diapers until she's in her eighties, that there really are moments of relief from the intensity of homework and school projects. I don't know if we comprehend the beauty of blessing we offer to women coming up behind us when we share our spiritual journey, when we join them in Bible study, when we tell them what we've learned in our walk with God, what we've learned as a wife, what we've learned as a mother in our years with the Lord.

When my kids were in their teens, I was part of a weekly Bible study with twelve women, half of whom were older than me by at least twenty years. Two of the women were widows in their nineties. I and the other younger women would moan and groan and cry about our kids—our struggles, our fears, our anxieties, our inadequacies, and our doubts. Precious Jeannette Hulin and Jan Bealer would empathetically listen to our heartaches and tales of woe. Then—without fail—they would respond with words of unshakable confidence in God and his character, speaking from faith grown solid and steady through decades of knowing and loving him. "Oh, honey," they would say, "don't you worry. God is good; he will not abandon you or your children. I've had some hard times too, but you can trust him no matter what."

Simple words spoken by women long past their prime in our youth-exalting culture, but words that carried me and the rest of our group through those years. Right in front of our eyes were two flesh-and-blood women whose seasoned trust in God made the Word come alive. They pooh-poohed our admiration, not out of false humility but because they simply couldn't believe that what they said made a difference to us. But dear Jeannette and Jan, as you watch now from heaven's glories, know that I haven't forgotten your words of encouragement and faith or your lives of commitment to Jesus. You poured strength into me and helped me believe I could be a good mom.

And so it is when we tenderly care for the generation coming behind us. They don't need experts or superstars. They need flesh-and-blood women who make God real.

Every season has limitations *and* opportunities. A wise woman stops fighting the limitations and consciously looks for ways to relish the opportunities of the living and breathing moments that are given to her.

⟶ **Enjoy the Moments** ⟵

We have an unfortunate tendency to focus anywhere but on the present. We can experience tremendous anxiety as we look ahead to the future. "What if this happens?" "How will I handle that situation?" It's easy to be consumed with what the future is going to look like and what we will do in certain scenarios and certain situations.

For others, the future isn't as anxiety producing as the past. Reliving our years of parenting sometimes leads to sadness because of missed opportunities, things we didn't do as well as we thought we should, or outright failure. Many long for a do-over. Sometimes we just get nostalgic for what once was. Even though it's been fifteen years since my kids were living at home, there are times I wish the house was filled again with the raucous sound of my teenagers and their friends giggling and playing games. I want to make them cupcakes with homemade buttercream icing and stand in the kitchen listening to their hopes and dreams and struggles. But those days are gone, and Rick and I "sit quietly by the fires and listen to the laughter in the walls."[3]

> *This* is the *moment* in which God can be *found*.

This is the moment you and I are responsible for. *This* is the moment in which God can be found. God reveals himself to us in the limitations *and* the opportunities of each season. Jim Elliot said, "Live to the hilt every situation you believe to be the will of God."[4]

If you wait for perfection, you'll miss too many moments. Do you know what that means? It means you go to your kid's or grandchild's baseball game even if you don't like baseball, and you make a fool of yourself by being the number one fan. You attend the ballet recital, and you clap for your little princess even if she forgot half of all she learned in the lessons you paid hard-earned dollars for. It means you tap your husband's shoulder as his eyes are glued to his computer screen and wait for him to look at you—and instead of complaining about the amount of time he's spending on the computer, you say, "I don't think I've told you yet today that I love you—but I do." It means you set the DVR for your favorite TV show and get cozy with your kids and read the book you've already read every day for a month straight. It means you call up a friend and say, "I'm up to my ears in mountains of laundry right now, but I miss you! Let's go grab a cup of coffee." It means you take a walk after work even though your body wants nothing more than a quick nap because the sunset is breathtaking and you get that *this* is a moment to relish.

Listen to me. The past is no longer yours. The future is not yours. All you have is this moment, and it is a gift from God. Every season is a gift—even if it is accompanied by hurt. If we begin each day with the awareness that we are called to live carefully, mindfully, wisely—with our eyes wide open to the opportunities found in this particular day—we will come closer to the lives God has planned for us.

May we passionately seek the opportunities hidden in each season, the joys unique to each one. May we be women of extraordinary wisdom who know how to love all the living and breathing moments we are given.

Protecting Your Private Life

Whatever weakens your reason, impairs the
tenderness of your conscience, obscures
your sense of God, or takes off the relish
for spiritual things then it is sin for you,
however innocent it may be in itself.

SUSANNAH WESLEY,
wife of John Wesley

Since Rick and I both grew up in the fishbowl atmosphere
of ministry homes, I thought I knew all there was about
living in the spotlight. I was fully aware that the congregation
and the community would watch us and our kids. I already knew
that people would be interested in the way we dressed, what
kind of cars we drove, the size of our house, what neighborhood we lived in, how much makeup I wore, where we sent our

kids to school, whether my children were well behaved, and if I looked sufficiently interested in Rick's sermons and laughed at his jokes. I thought our life would look very much like that of our parents and felt I was ready and equipped to handle any privacy curveballs ministry could throw at me.

What I didn't know was that Saddleback was going to become a really big church in a rather small area—10 percent of the population of Saddleback Valley attends our church—which means we run into people who recognize us every time we walk out our door. My dad pastored small churches in San Diego, and we never ran into church members when we went out, so this was a huge adjustment. I didn't know that Rick would gain such attention from writing *The Purpose Driven Life* and that someday people would go through our trash and use a telephoto lens from the canyon behind our house to try to get a closer look at us. It's probably a good thing I didn't know what was ahead of us when we started Saddleback with seven people in our condo in 1980.

I could either get mad about our loss of privacy and focus on the negatives of being public people, or I could decide we're going to live graciously and with unquestionable integrity. You know where I'm going to land. Here are two ways I've learned to maintain a private life as a public person that I think will apply to anyone living in the glare of the spotlight of a ministry home.

Accept the Loss of Privacy with God's Grace

I decided a long time ago that I was going to accept the loss of privacy with grace. I have accepted the reality that our family is an object of interest and to some degree we're fair game when we're out in public. I've chosen to ignore paranoid thoughts—*These people are spies and stalkers and they're following us*—and reframe the situation in my mind: *They're just people who love us and love our church, and to them, our family is an object of interest.* As I said, you can walk around with a big chip on your shoulder and resent that you're an object of interest, or you can learn how to gracefully accept a smaller measure of privacy than the typical family. By the way, your kids will take their cues from you. If you get bent out of shape when someone stops you at the mall, expect your kids to get bent out of shape. If you model grace and kindness, they're more likely to be gracious as well.

One of the ways I cope is to use humor. If I can laugh about something, it keeps me from getting annoyed. I'd love to swap stories with you about the ways the public has intruded into your private life. I'll bet your stories can top mine. We've done a lot of life in this valley over the last thirty-six years, and here are a few of my favorites:

- The time I was really late getting my kids to school and hopped in the car wearing pj's, slippers, and no bra—and ran out of gas on the side of the freeway. As I recall, the sheriff's deputy who stopped to help me went to Saddleback.

- The time I was coming out of anesthesia after back surgery to find a male nurse helping me onto the bedpan with the words, "I love to see you singing in the choir." I didn't have coherent words to tell him I don't sing in the choir; it was enough to know he thought he had seen me there and was now going to be imagining me on a bedpan.

- The time the nurse in the colonoscopy lab told me she attends Saddleback right as I was counting backward from ten to one. Before I was out like a light, I had five seconds of hoping I had done a good job of prepping for the test and that her shift would be over before I woke up. When I woke up, I was too groggy to care how much of my private life she had seen.

- The time we were in England doing the tourist thing in Warwick Castle when a man caught a glimpse of Rick and shouted across the length of an enormous dining room full of other tourists, "Hey, is that you, Pastor Rick?" Sometimes I get snarky and think to myself, *No, it's his evil twin, Mick.*

- The time I was unloading ice cream from my grocery cart onto the conveyor belt and the woman behind me said loudly with great displeasure, "Should Pastor Rick be eating that?" I try to tell him to keep his weight-loss efforts to himself so I don't have to deal with judgmental church members in the grocery store.

- The time three little old ladies gathered around me after a service and said, "We just love to see what you're wearing each week." Something really naughty in me wanted to make a smart-aleck comment about underwear, but I kept my mouth shut and just smiled.

- The time a young man having a psychotic break kept banging on our front door, putting his eye up to the security camera on the porch so that all I could see from the inside was a gigantic eyeball. He urgently repeated, "Tell Pastor Rick I got his message and I'm ready to join the fight!"

Poor guy. I hated to call 911, but he was prepared to camp out on my porch indefinitely, waiting to be a part of Rick's "fight," whatever that was.

I especially wasn't prepared for the thousands of small encounters over the years—the times people walked up to our table in a restaurant and said, "I don't want to interrupt your family time," and then proceeded to do just that. Or the zillions of times people saw Rick in a store and said, "Could I have just a minute of your time? I've always wanted to pick your brain about . . ." Rick says it's no wonder he can't remember anything anymore because his brain has been picked clean. We always try to be gracious, but there have been a few moments when we just wanted to be invisible and buy the bag of fertilizer we came to Home Depot to buy.

You have to laugh—or cry—at the absurdity of it all. I mean, whoever thought a *pastor's* family would be the cause of so much commotion? Laughter eases the tension of being in the public eye and can make you and your family coconspirators—meaning the shared experiences of being objects of interest can become fodder for family stories and legends that get repeated endlessly throughout the years. We have some private jokes about a few of our encounters with the public, and we laugh uproariously every time they're mentioned. They have become a part of what binds us together.

Edith Schaeffer, cofounder of L'Abri, gives a poetic definition of a family in *What Is a Family?*:

> A family is a door that has hinges and a lock. The hinges should be well-oiled to swing the door open during certain times, but the lock should be firm enough to let people know that the family

needs to be alone part of the time, just to be a family. If a family is to be really shared, then there needs to be something to share.[1]

As a family, keep in mind you're an object of interest and allow the door to swing open at times. When you go out in public, people will see you and want to talk to you. But you do have the right to a private life, and there are many more times when the door needs to swing shut so that you are protected from the public eye and are by yourselves to be a family.

Our grandkids are growing up and starting to deal with the awareness that their family is different, and our kids and their spouses now have the task of preparing their children for life in the spotlight. Papa can inadvertently create quite a stir when he shows up at their school events and the news starts traveling. I love it when I see the older grandkids shrug it off when adults and even kids want to speak to Rick and even ask for photos. Most of the time they don't mind the attention given to their grandparents or parents, but I'm not going to lie. It's not easy, and it's not always comfortable for them. Plenty of times it's a struggle not to get annoyed or irritated by the constant eyes on us, times when the grandkids want to know they're just kids—not Rick Warren's grandkids. Part of what we pass on to the next generation is modeling how to accept the loss of privacy with God's grace, completely depending on him for kindness and patience when it's rough.

I know people are looking at me. I've accepted that reality. Once I made peace with that, I decided I was going to leverage their interest for the kingdom of God, to use my visibility as an inspiration and influence for good. When people look at me, I want them to be able to say, "Oh, so that's what it means to love Jesus in the hard times." Or "So that's what it looks like to be a team in ministry with your husband." Or "So that's what it looks like to love your kids unconditionally." Of course, this is a delicate dance. I want to live authentically, out of the constrictive box of faking it and trying to please people, but at the same time I want to live with the awareness that I can model the faith I profess in my daily interactions with a watching world. Thinking of the ways I can use my visibility in positive ways helps me on the days I just want to pick up a prescription at the drugstore without having to be "on."

There will likely be periods in your life when being in the public eye is particularly burdensome. It might be due to a higher than normal level of stress, something one of your kids is going through, conflict in the church, or your health. There are so many reasons for needing more privacy. For most of the years at Saddleback, I've sat off to the side of the stage in the front row because Rick likes to see me when he's preaching. I think it's so he can instantly beg forgiveness for saying something I'm going to disapprove of, but he assures me it's because my presence is such an encouragement to him. When he catches my eye, he says it gives him strength on the days he's extra tired. But when Matthew died, being in the public eye was excruciating for me. I knew I would eventually settle into my commitment to leverage my visibility for God's kingdom, but it wouldn't be anytime soon. I couldn't bear to know I was being watched and evaluated. I didn't go to church at all for four months. I barely left the house except to see my family or go to the cemetery. When I went back to church, I switched to the service my kids and grandkids attended so I could be one of a group, not a lone person in the front row. I would wait until the service began and then slip into the back row as unobtrusively as possible, making sure I had safe people—family, friends, or small group members—on every side. If I couldn't handle being in a sensory-stimulating environment on a particular day, I would just leave. I usually left before the last amen anyway so that I didn't have to engage in casual conversation with strangers or even familiar people; it was just too much.

It was a year and a half before I was ready to sit in the front row again—and if I had needed longer, I would have taken it. I felt no guilt for needing more privacy during the initial months of grief. No one could have made me do it any differently. When *I* felt I was ready—not when church members wanted to see me in my usual spot—I made the decision to try it. My sister-in-love, Chaundel, and my dear friend Joy were a gentle presence around me. I'm so glad I waited. Now when the lyrics of a song, the emotional tie to a song I've loved for a long time, or no clear reason at all brings tears, I let them come. Publicly. Sitting in the front row. Sometimes alone. It's healthy to mourn and grieve in community—to unashamedly express sorrow and hope. My arms raised in worship, body moving, tears flowing, sometimes laughter and smiles in response to praising Jesus—these actions reveal what I believe to anyone watching or observing: God is good and I trust him.

> We make him *known* by our lives—public and private.

As pastors' families, we're not just objects of interest. We're also living object lessons to a watching congregation, neighborhood, and extended family about who God is. We make him known by our lives—public and private.

Seek an Integrated Life

You are entitled to a private life. But while you have the right to a private life, you don't have the right to private sins. Sadly, we've all seen the fallout when well-known Christians who preached hard against sin had their own secret sins exposed.

After the early years of hiding our brokenness, Rick and I decided we were going to invest in integrity in a way that would allow our public and private lives to match as much as possible. We know the two will never match up perfectly because we're never going to get it right all the time—this is earth, not heaven! But it is our intention to be the same in private as we are in public.

What happens too many times to people in ministry is that somewhere along the way a gap develops between what is said and lived in public and what is said and lived in private. Maybe you and your husband are having conflict in your marriage, and you don't know how to change the unhealthy patterns of relating. Perhaps one of you is drinking too much or has become addicted to prescription painkillers to deal with the stress and pressure of your life. You might suspect your husband is too attached to another woman in the church, but he denies it; meanwhile, your marriage is tanking. Your child might have mental or physical health issues; struggles in school; or problems with drugs, alcohol, sex, or pornography. Perhaps your finances—the lack of or the mismanagement of—are creating sleepless nights for you. It's possible emotional or physical abuse is happening between you and your husband or between you and one of your kids. You don't tell anyone because you keep thinking things will level out or the wrong behavior will stop or you'll think of a solution, but the situation is getting worse. Nobody starts off intending to lead a double life, but it's easier than you realize to wake up one morning to the shocking revelation that there is a Grand Canyon–sized gap between your private life and your public life.

If your goal is to integrate your private life and your public life, you'll have to start sharing what is going on behind closed doors. We reveal our brokenness, our weaknesses, our temptations, our failures, and our junk so that integration becomes possible. None of us will ever do it perfectly. We've all got stuff we're working on. There's a difference, though, between seasons of struggle and perennial habits that become a way of life. When what you're presenting to the world is vastly different from what is really true—the gap between public and private is getting bigger and bigger rather than smaller and smaller—it's time to push the pause button on ministry and say, "I need help."

If one of you is having an emotional and/or sexual affair, you will have to take radical steps to get your lives back on track. A return to wholeness and health starts with telling the truth about your lives and being willing to do whatever it takes to mend and repair what has been shattered between you. You won't be able to fix this by yourselves—and moreover, you shouldn't even try. Our quest for integrity and the integration of public and private can happen only in safe community with others committed to integrity and integration.

There is rarely a single solution to our complex problems, so reach out in every direction: seek spiritual guidance and advice from trusted believers; get a complete physical from your doctor; confess the good, the bad, and the ugly to a close friend or family member; join a small group or ministry support group;

lean hard on your relationship with Jesus; take stock of where you've gotten lax in tending to your body, soul, and spirit; get counseling; and for many, join Celebrate Recovery. Celebrate Recovery (CR) is a Christian twelve-step program started at Saddleback in 1991 and is used by more than two million Christians around the world, not just for alcohol or drug addiction but for any hurt, habit, or hang-up that is negatively affecting them. There's even a subset of CR called CPR—Celebrate Pastors' Recovery—and there are dozens of these groups around the country for people in ministry (go to www.cprpastors.com to find a group in your area).

This entire conversation strikes fear in the hearts of some of you; this is exactly where you're caught. You've been paddling as fast as you can to keep things afloat, to prop up your marriage or your children, hoping you're doing an okay job of keeping the bad stuff under wraps and that no one will notice the discrepancy between your private and public lives. You are on high alert. It's exhausting, isn't it? How long do you think you can keep everything hidden? A better question is, wouldn't you like some relief?

> How long do you think you can keep everything *hidden*? A better question is, wouldn't you like some *relief*?

I need to tell you that eventually "it" will come to light. Whatever it is you're hiding will pop to the surface. The lies you're telling to protect yourself or your family will be revealed; stories and people crack wide open after a while. The truth gets out—it always gets out. It might take a long time, but all will be found out at some point. I lived with too many secrets and can tell you from personal experience that the phrase "it eats at you" is accurate. In CR, people say, "You're only as sick as your secrets." Secrets, unconfessed sin, and hidden struggles have the power to make you physically ill. They can erode emotional and mental health. They certainly diminish your intimacy with God. Please don't wait any longer to get help. The issue isn't whether or not you have a completely healthy, intact, and functional family but what you do about the stress, conflict, and dysfunction. Hiding it, ignoring it, pretending it doesn't exist, denying there's a problem, or blaming your husband or your children or the church members for your unhappiness is not the solution. Getting help is the solution. Getting help when you're in ministry is scary—so much is at stake—but you are not weird or truly messed up if you need to ask for outside help. You are not alone.

Paul's Model of Integrity

Second Corinthians is the go-to book in the Bible if you want to study a model of living authentically in ministry. I try to read it at least once a year because it inspires me to keep on seeking to live with integrity. Let's take a look at a few of the key verses and the responses I believe are called for.

1. I will aim for a clear conscience, seeking to live with holiness, integrity, and sincerity.

> Now this is our boast: Our conscience testifies that we have conducted ourselves in the world, and especially in our relations with you, with integrity and godly sincerity. We have done so, relying not on worldly wisdom but on God's grace. (2 Cor. 1:12)

Paul makes no bones about it. His stated goal was to bring honor to the Lord by the way he lived.

2. I realize my audience is God and will speak truthfully and sincerely.

> You see, we are not like the many hucksters who preach for personal profit. We preach the word of God with sincerity and with Christ's authority, knowing that God is watching us. (2 Cor. 2:17 NLT)

Your audience is God, and he cannot be fooled. You may be able to fool your husband. You may be able to fool your kids. You may be able to fool your small group. You may be able to fool the people in your ministry. Really, we're pretty good at fooling people, but we can't put one over on God. He knows it all. In light of his all-seeing eye, we need to speak truthfully and with sincerity.

3. I will remember that ministry is a sacred privilege and will get rid of secret, shameful sins.

> Therefore, since through God's mercy we have this ministry, we do not lose heart. Rather, we have renounced secret and shameful ways; we do not use deception, nor do we distort the word of God. On the contrary, by setting forth the truth plainly we commend ourselves to everyone's conscience in the sight of God. (2 Cor. 4:1–2)

None of us deserve to be in ministry. None of us even deserve to be Christians. It's truly by God's grace that we're believers in Christ and that he's accepted us into his family. You're not in ministry because you are an amazing person the world can't live without. You are in ministry because of God's grace; he chose to allow you to be in this position. In recognition of the privilege and God-given honor, we need to renounce any secret and shameful ways and live with integrity.

4. I will make every effort to have my private and public lives match—no hiding or pretending.

> We know what it means to respect the Lord, and we encourage everyone to turn to him. God himself knows what we are like, and I hope you also know what kind of people we are. (2 Cor. 5:11 CEV)

Paul says, "What you see is what you get." When you see me, Paul says, my public and private lives match, as much as is humanly possible. People always ask, "What is Rick like in private?" I think he's exactly the same (for better or worse) in private as he is in public—only more so! He's goofy. He's funny. He's wise. He's brilliant. He's simple. He is who he is. He doesn't pretend to be warm and loving in public and then is a cold fish in private. There has never been a gap between the public and the private man. Paul is saying, "What we are is plainly visible to all."

5. I will keep in mind how easy it is to discredit the ministry by my behavior and lifestyle.

> We put no obstruction in anybody's way [we give no offense in anything], so that no fault may be found and [our] ministry blamed and discredited. (2 Cor. 6:3 AMP-CE)

Paul says our behavior can offend people, giving them a reason to discredit the ministry. Other versions say that our behavior can actually be an obstacle or a stumbling block to people coming to Christ. Paul says, "I get it. It doesn't take much to discredit God and the ministry." Verses 4–10 detail the enormous effort he put into doing the exact opposite—all the ways he attempted to make it easier for people to come to know Christ—and every one of them was about his behavior or his response to trouble. According to Paul, whether beaten, imprisoned, starved, or criticized, we show ourselves to be true servants of God by our integrity, purity, honesty, and genuine lives.

One of the saddest things about being in ministry for more than forty years is seeing the road littered with the lives of people we knew in college and seminary. These are people who loved Jesus, had a passion and a calling for ministry, and yet somehow they made a series of mistakes that led to a moral failure of some sort. Most of the time they failed in one of the three areas in which Satan always sets traps: sex, money, power.

Rick actually has a "warnings" file. I call it the "scare the crud out of me" file. When he hears of people we know or well-known pastors who leave ministry because they failed in one of these areas, he sticks them in his file. We regularly read that file together because we understand that the ministry can be so easily discredited and we don't want to put a stumbling block in the way of people who are seeking God. Who gets hurt when ministers fail to live up to standards of integrity? A watching world mocks us, mocks the church, and mocks God, but God takes the biggest hit because of our stupidity. God is the one who gets hurt the most when ministers fail. I can't be responsible for that. My life is going to be authentic, and I'm going to live with integrity.

This might sound overly dramatic, but it comes from the deepest part of my soul—if there is ever too big a gap between my private life and my public life, I hope I get out of the way because I do not ever want to hurt the name of Jesus Christ.

6. I will get rid of anything that contaminates my body or my spirit.

> Since we have these promises, dear friends, we need to cleanse ourselves from everything that contaminates body and spirit and live a holy life in the fear of God. (2 Cor. 7:1 GW)

Paul recognizes there are some sins that contaminate our bodies. There are some sins that contaminate our spirits. Paul says he's staying away from anything that can make him impure.

7. Everything in my life—including my finances—is in order. I will live with transparency and work hard to do what is right in the sight of God and others.

> What is more, he was chosen by the churches to accompany us as we carry the offering, which we administer in order to honor the Lord himself and to show our eagerness to help. We want to avoid any criticism of the way we administer this liberal gift. For we are taking pains to do what is right, not only in the eyes of the Lord but also in the eyes of man. (2 Cor. 8:19–21)

As you know, finances are one of the three common places of stumbling for the clergy. I guess it's always been that way because Paul assured the Corinthians that he and his team were being extremely careful with the financial gift entrusted to them. It sounds to me as if they went way beyond what might have been considered appropriate in handling the money in a correct way—he wasn't going to allow even the slightest hint of impropriety to create suspicion. Oh, that more pastors were as careful as Paul! I cannot advise you strongly enough not to touch the money. Make sure you know where it's going and who's responsible for it, but don't touch it yourself. How many times have you heard of a pastor who "borrowed" money from the church's bank account with the intention of paying it back before it was discovered missing only to get caught? Or equally sad is the pastor who takes money to pay for items he can't afford without any intention of paying it back. The sins of pastors everywhere hurt all of us, but in the end, God's reputation takes the biggest hit.

> I cannot advise you strongly enough not to touch the *money*.

Two Cautions

If you find yourself looking with contempt at other people who have fallen and think, *I would never do that*, please consider the following.

First, in misunderstanding the depth of your own depravity, you are in effect waving a big red flag to our enemy that says, "Come get me." We don't like to admit it, but the truth is, given the right circumstances, anyone can commit *any* sin. Don't protest too strongly. Your pride is setting you up for ruin. Proverbs 16:18 says, "Pride precedes a disaster, and an arrogant attitude precedes a fall" (GW).

Rick recently told a ministry friend seeking advice, "Always do the humiliating thing—the thing that makes you the most humble—because God gives grace to the humble." We must have humble hearts if we want God's healing for our brokenness.

Second, by harshly condemning the sin of another believer without offering the grace that comes from knowing you are just one stupid mistake away from being in the same boat, you are asking to be judged with the same harshness for your sins.

Matthew 7:1–2 says, "Do not judge, or you too will be judged. For in the same way you judge others, you will be judged, and with the measure you use, it will be measured to you." These verses are conveniently trotted out by many who think the point is that no one should ever be called on the carpet for their actions. That is *not* what Jesus is saying. Too many other verses in the Bible clearly teach righteous and holy living. In the verses that follow, Jesus uses hyperbole to point out the deadly vice of pride and how it blinds us to ourselves—so much so that we can walk around with a two-by-four in our eye while yelling at our neighbor for having a speck of sawdust in theirs. His message is this: "Sin is really serious. Be aware that as you point out your neighbor's sin, I'm taking notice of yours as well. No one is immune. I'm not giving you a pass to sin even more freely. I'm telling you to be sure your own heart is clean and pure as you speak about your sister's or brother's failings."

François Fénelon, a seventeenth-century French Catholic bishop, writes:

> When you become outraged over a person's fault, it is generally not "righteous indignation" but your own impatient personality expressing itself. Here is the imperfect pointing a finger at the imperfect. The more you selfishly love yourself the more critical you will be. Self-love cannot forgive the self-love it discovers in others. Nothing is so offensive to a haughty, conceited heart as the sight of another one.[2]

━━ Follow Me as I Follow Christ ━━

You're not entitled to private sins, but you are entitled to a private life.

With God's help, you can choose to accept the loss of privacy and model for your children how to live graciously and freely, finding humor where possible in your fishbowl existence. You can learn how to draw boundaries around times in public and times that are just for the intimacy of your family.

My prayer for you is that you will courageously decide you're done with a double life. You're through pretending and hiding and covering up and lying. You're more interested in bringing your public and your private lives back together—to close the gap—so you can live whole and healthy lives.

Yes, people will watch you—that isn't going to stop. Don't forget you can leverage your visibility to be a positive influence and to inspire those who are watching. We can show by our lives that God is good and that he can be trusted even in the darkest times. This is a motto I heard from a fellow pastor's wife, Devi Titus, and I adopted it as an introverted, shy, young pastor's wife struggling to find her way: "So look on! Evaluate me, scrutinize me. Criticize me if you feel you're justified. And if you see me following Christ, then follow me!"[3]

Will you leave a path for others to follow? Or will you end up in somebody's "warnings file"? It doesn't have to be that way. You can choose.

10

Dealing with Criticism

Now, Friends, deal plainly with yourselves, and let the eternal Light search you, and try you, for the good of your souls. For this will deal plainly with you. It will rip you up, and lay you open, and make all manifest which lodges in you; the secret subtlety of the enemy of your souls, this eternal searcher and trier will make manifest. Therefore all to this come, and by this be searched, and judged, and led and guided. For to this you must stand or fall.

MARGARET FELL,
wife of George Fox

As we talk about challenges that happen over the years in ministry, another area to be aware of is criticism. I wish I could say that criticism is rare and you probably don't have to worry about it, but it comes with the territory. At some level, it happens to all of us. Through the years Rick has been able to handle criticism easier than I have. His typical response is, "What's wrong with *you*?" while my typical response is, "What's wrong with *us*? What have *we* done wrong?" I've had to mature in my ability to process criticism in healthy ways.

Criticism comes in a myriad of forms, from a disapproving look to whisper campaigns to overt negative comments. At times, the criticism escalates to open conflict and occasionally to a full-on attack in which members leave the church en masse and the church splits. Sometimes criticism culminates in your husband being asked or forced to leave. It's undoubtedly the worst part of ministry, and if you've been on the receiving end of it, you can probably point to the scars that remain.

What causes criticism? So many possibilities: traditions challenged, fear of change, immaturity, sin, spiritual warfare, poor leadership, financial concerns, poor fit between pastor and congregation, inadequate communication, personality clashes, gossip, lack of grace and forgiveness, differing visions for the future. All of these and many others can factor into the painful wounds of criticism and conflict.

Sadly, church conflict has the power to wound and damage those involved in almost the same way as a family that fractures and eventually disintegrates into divorce, leaving each family member ripped and torn inside. That shouldn't surprise us because we are a spiritual family; the Bible refers to the church as God's family in 1 Timothy 3:15: "I want you to know how people who are members of God's family must live. God's family is the church of the living God, the pillar and foundation of the truth" (GW).

So we're not only a body of inter-related and dependent parts (Rom. 12:5) but also a family that is held together by commitments and loyalties and vows. Like human families, the church is made up of human beings who are all in process; in the case of the church, we're in the process of being made holy. We're all on the road to becoming Christlike, spiritually healthy, and mature, but that process is often slow and chaotic; it can get downright ugly. And when a person in process messes up, the situation always spills over onto others.

> Sadly, church *conflict* has the power to wound and damage those involved in almost the same way as a *family* that fractures and eventually disintegrates into divorce.

═══ Outside the Church ═══

Sometimes criticism comes from the outside. We have received a fair amount of criticism through the years, starting from day one of Saddleback Church. When we launched Saddleback, we weren't trying to be radical heretics. We weren't trying to be rabble-rousers and cause trouble or make a name for ourselves. From the depths of our hearts, our motivation was to reach unchurched people in this valley where we live. We weren't interested in stealing people from existing churches—our target was people who weren't going to *any* church. Our only thought was how to capture their hearts and their attention long enough for them to hear the message that God loves them. If that meant doing things in a slightly unorthodox way, then so be it. The goal—bring unsaved men, women, boys, and girls into a relationship with Jesus Christ and into the warm fellowship of his body—was simple and clear, and we were willing to risk it all on their behalf. We still are.

In the 1980s, most churches still wore a denominational label; "community churches" were rare and a cause for suspicion among those in established denominations. Thirty-six years later, you can call your church anything and no one blinks an eye, but we took a lot of heat initially for not calling ourselves Saddleback Valley Southern Baptist Church. How could we abandon our heritage? Did we think we were better than everybody else? Did we even still love Jesus? People screamed bloody murder—like we'd advocated lining up Southern Baptists as a whole and tossing them over a cliff. We were stung by the knee-jerk reactions and accusations hurled at us by some; the ones that stung the most were from people who knew us and should have known our hearts.

Looking back, that was the kindergarten level of criticism. We've accumulated a lot of vitriol since 1980. People have said—and continue to say—much worse things about us than those early denunciations, from calling us "gospel lite" to "false prophets" to "proponents of Chrislam" to the "antichrist" (yeah, who can forget the son of a well-known TV evangelist who ranted into the camera that Rick Warren was part of the antichrist, that he needed to come under the blood of the Lamb, and that *The Purpose Driven Life* should not be read because it was full of lies straight from the pit of hell?). Rick is usually the target of these comments

> I'm dumbfounded by the amount of vulgarity and obscenity even *Christians* can use when criticizing one another.

because he is highly visible as the lead pastor. I'll never forget the first time cruel comments were directed at me when I became an advocate for people living with HIV. I received an email from an angry person who said, "I wish you had died of breast cancer." Sigh. Those are just a sampling of the G-rated comments. We've received hundreds of other comments that aren't fit to read or print. I'm dumbfounded by the amount of vulgarity and obscenity even Christians can use when criticizing one another.

Inside the Church

"Professional" criticism—critiques about our work, our ministry, the way we do church—from outside the church is painful, but the most painful criticism always comes from church members, co-workers in the Lord, and friends—people we dearly love. People for whom we've sacrificed time, energy, money, and passion. People we've served closely with in ministry. People for whom we've shown up for the births, graduations, weddings, and funerals of their lives. You just can't please everybody, and it is exhausting to try. People don't always understand the backstory of personnel changes or appreciate the hours your team spent on their knees seeking God before announcing a vision change, and they respond with doubts, confusion, and even outright hostility. Sometimes the criticism is hot and heavy and intense—and unfortunately, very, very personal. When church members receive your love and care and then stab you in the back, they can create wounds so deep it feels as though they'll never heal. This type of criticism can suck the life out of you, leaving you bitter and disillusioned, ready to abandon ministry entirely.

Saddleback is by and large a grace-filled place, but even with deep bonds of love between us and our members, there have been a couple of occasions when disgruntled people got upset, stirred up animosity, and left the church, taking others with them. We intimately knew and loved the people involved. We were devastated to lose these key families, and I remember shedding many tears. Rick and I analyzed our actions, our words, and our behavior and felt we had been in the right, but in one sense, it didn't matter who was right or who was wrong. The unity and harmony of our church had been damaged, people we cared about were broken, and we grieved deeply. I lost the friendship of someone very dear to me—a close co-worker in ministry I loved. She was angry and felt wronged. I was angry and felt wronged. Talking about it or trying to work it out went nowhere. There was just suddenly a hole where our friendship had been. It took many years for healing to occur, but it did—and I'm so grateful.

Another time criticism stung badly was when a spiritually mature couple joined the church and the wife became a leader in our fledgling women's ministry. She had vast biblical knowledge and years of experience leading women. We connected almost immediately, and she became not only a friend but also a wise mentor I looked up to. She came from a church very different from Saddleback—much more traditional with a heavy emphasis on verse-by-verse Bible preaching as the *correct* (read "only") way to preach. Looking back, I'm not really sure why they even gave Saddleback a try, but they were with us for a few years.

One day my friend and mentor announced they were leaving and going to a church where they "preach the Bible." I was devastated and humiliated by her words; she made me feel as if we were spiritually beneath her. There was no talking them out of their decision to leave. They resigned their leadership positions immediately and left. I think I've seen her only once in the many years since, and when we did run into each other, it was painful and awkward—at least for me. I don't think she ever knew how badly her criticism hurt me or how much I grieved the loss of an older woman I loved and respected. I've often wondered how much good they could have done if they had been patient with our young church and young leadership, how much benefit we would have gained from their experience.

The stories I've heard from pastors and their families over the years would break your heart. I could write a book on this subject alone. Some have endured almost unimaginable injuries from churches they've served. Occasionally, differences are ironed out, restitution and reconciliation take place, and the wounded members return and serve with their whole hearts. But most of the time weeks, months, and years go by with no reconciliation, and the losses add up.

There are only three ways I know to survive and recover from criticism, complaints, conflicts, and the resulting wounds: leave the results to God, be grateful for the positive side of ministry, and practice radical forgiveness.

——— Leave the Results to God ———

When we plant a church or start at a new church, we often ask ourselves, "Can we make this succeed? Can we make a go of this?" After we've been there a while, the question shifts to, "How long can we maintain this?" The pressure to do well increases over time, and so can the criticism. Sometimes criticism is like the constant drip of a leaky faucet, but other times—as in Acts 5:17–42—the opposition is fierce.

Acts 5:17–42 records a conversation between an influential religious leader of his day, Gamaliel, and other prominent members of the Jewish Sanhedrin who were angry at the apostle Peter and the other apostles. The apostles were causing an uproar in Jerusalem with their teaching about Jesus and their healing of many sick people in his name. Gamaliel calmed the religious leaders down with his sage advice in verses 38–39:

> Therefore, in the present case I advise you: Leave these men alone! Let them go! For if their purpose or activity is of human origin, it will fail. But if it is from God, you will not be able to stop these men; you will only find yourselves fighting against God.

Gamaliel pointed out that when God is behind something, nothing any human being does can interrupt his plan. I have drawn strength and courage from this verse many times.

Our rule of thumb about criticism is to ask, "Is there any truth to it?" This is the humble part of leadership—being willing to consider the possibility that there might be a few grains of truth in someone's complaint or criticism. Humility is especially required if the criticism is coming from a person you don't like or respect or agree with. But if there's any truth at all, receive it, apply it, and make the necessary changes. Be ready to apologize if appropriate. If the criticism is not true, then treat it the same way you eat a fish: eat the meat and throw away the bones. Let it go. Don't get bogged down in the small stuff. You've got a God to serve, a husband and kids and maybe grandkids to love, and ministry to do. Don't get caught in the trap of trying to make everybody happy.

Don't take criticism personally. When people used to tell us they were leaving Saddleback because of this or that, it hurt me deeply. Most of the time I'm now able to say, "We're so glad you've been here. I hope you enjoy the next place God sends you and that you will quickly feel at home there."

With that said, there might be times in your ministry when you're doing everything right as far as you can tell. You're as surrendered to God as you know how to be, you're walking by faith, you're dreaming great dreams for the kingdom, and yet terrible opposition from within your congregation is building. From your perspective, you're not doing anything wrong or against God. But conflict develops, congregational dissatisfaction grows, and before you know it, you're facing either dismissal or voluntary resignation. It's tempting to beat yourself up or point the finger at your spouse. But here's what I want you to remember: a lack of visible blessing from God does not automatically mean you've sinned or failed; sometimes the failure is someone else's. Congregations can miss the mark as well. Here are three possibilities:

Don't get *caught* in the trap of trying to make everybody *happy*.

- Sometimes we get off track; our efforts fall short, and it's obvious to all.
- Sometimes we are on track and nothing can stop us.
- Sometimes we are on track but failure happens anyway.

The comfort you can take from Acts 5:38–39 is this: If your approach to ministry is of God, it will be okay. If it is not of God, it will fail. And it will be okay that way too. Either way, God is at work in your life. If you're right on track with his plan, the criticism and opposition won't be able to derail you. If you've done something that wasn't according to God's plan, he will use the failure to gently teach you and restore you and bring you into another season of ministry. He is still working out his plan of love in your life and ministry. It just might not look the way you planned.

——— Be Grateful for the Positive Side of Ministry ———

In my nonscientific survey of three thousand pastors' wives who follow me or Rick on social media, 77 percent of the respondents rated their experience as a pastor's wife as positive to very positive (10 percent rated it 6 out of 10; 23 percent rated it 7 out of 10; 25 percent rated it 8 out of 10; 11 percent rated it 9 out of 10; and 8 percent rated it 10 out of 10). Thirteen percent rated their experience as neutral, and ten percent of the respondents feel it is more negative than positive.

Some of the comments reflect the ambivalence many pastors' wives feel:

> I love getting a front row seat to what God is doing. The hard part of it is how many people want a piece of my husband and of me; it's difficult to manage it all.

> It's hard when your life is tied to the place where you're in community with people. This is where we have friends, a small group, and our family is engaged. At one point, there was a difference in opinion and we weren't sure what our future held.

When Rick was in seminary, we were in a church that had about seven hundred seminary couples, and the senior pastor's wife, Mary Burleson, really had a heart for those of us who were seminary wives. She taught a weekly class for us, passing on the wisdom she had gleaned in her decades of ministry. I've never forgotten one week's homework. We were to write down everything we could possibly think of that was positive about being in the ministry because, as Mary told us, there would be days we would hate the ministry and wish we were doing something else. She had us read Hebrews 12:15 together and said that if we learned to be grateful for the good things, it would protect us from becoming bitter.

> Look after each other so that not one of you will fail to find God's best blessings. Watch out that no bitterness takes root among you, for as it springs up it causes deep trouble, hurting many in their spiritual lives. (TLB)

The Phillips paraphrase says it like this:

> Be careful that none of you fails to respond to the grace which God gives, for if he does there can very easily spring up in him a bitter spirit which is not only bad in itself but can also poison the lives of many others.

We shared our personal lists with one another, compiling at least one hundred large and small positive aspects of being in the ministry. Here are just a few from the list: you can make great friendships; the environment is Bible centered; the meetings are smoke-free and alcohol-free; I work with people who share similar values; our children are exposed to people with strong character; there are people who minister to us; your labor is not in vain; you have an opportunity to have godly people in your home; you're aware of what's going on in the church; you can make your children feel special and important; your family can have a united purpose in ministry together; you can see God working and changing people's lives; there is a nurturing atmosphere in case of difficulties; you have the prayer support of many people.

Mary said, "Hold on to this list—keep it in your Bible—and on those really bad days, pull it out and remind yourself of the blessings that are yours." I still have my torn, dog-eared list.

I can't tell you how many times through the years I have dug out those pieces of paper and reviewed them in God's presence. Thank you, Mary.

> Every *positive* item will increase your *gratitude* and decrease the real possibility of bitterness twisting your soul.

Perhaps you've gotten a bit jaded or cynical about being in the ministry. The idiosyncrasies, faults, and sins of church members are wearing on you. Maybe criticism and opposition are in full swing right now. Maybe *any* career but the ministry looks appealing today. It might be time to compile a list of your own. Get your whole family engaged. Brainstorm together about the positives. Write them all down, even the silly responses such as, "I get donuts after church." Every positive item will increase your gratitude and decrease the real possibility of bitterness twisting your soul.

Practice Radical Forgiveness

Radical forgiveness will be required many times in your years of ministry. You will need to ask for it, and you will need to offer it. You're a fallible human being, and so are the people who sit in the pews. You're bound to mess up, and so are they.

You're familiar with the forgiveness verses in the Bible. You could probably quote five of them right now. You and I don't have trouble with forgiveness because we're unaware of what God says about it. It's not our ignorance that gets in the way. So why is it so ridiculously hard to truly, radically forgive someone in the church? Maybe the hurt catches us off guard when it comes from a fellow believer, as it did with King David in Psalm 55:12–14:

> It is not an enemy who taunts me—
>   I could bear that.
> It is not my foes who so arrogantly insult me—
>   I could have hidden from them.
> Instead, it is you—my equal,
>   my companion and close friend.
> What good fellowship we once enjoyed
>   as we walked together to the house of God. (NLT)

Recently, one of the charter members of the church who had been with us for thirty-five years passed away. Funerals can be challenging these days, and I particularly felt the sadness of saying good-bye to this beautiful, faithful woman of God. I planned to go to the cemetery for the burial following the memorial service, so I stopped to buy flowers for her gravesite as well as for Matthew's since he is buried in the same place.

As I walked up to the entrance of the grocery store where I intended to purchase the flowers, I noticed a man soliciting money for an organization. I usually give to whoever is there—Girl Scouts, Boy Scouts, Salvation Army—but this day I was in the grief zone. I stared at the ground, lost in my thoughts of grief for my friend and for Matthew. When the man asked if I would care to donate, I quickly looked up through my tears and said, "Not today, thank you." I went in, bought the flowers, and left the store.

Two days later I got a letter from that man. He said, "I was the one asking for donations in front of the market the other day and I noticed you did not give to this worthy cause and you gave me a dirty look. You should be careful because people are watching your life. I won't gossip about it, but you have a lot of money and you should have made a contribution."

Many times I can handle criticism with grace, but this time really made me mad. I think his words stung because he made an assumption about me in the middle of a grieving moment and then questioned my generosity. To top it off, he made a veiled threat about spreading a rumor about my supposed lack of generosity. I usually ignore letters like his or write back in a completely neutral and conciliatory tone without taking offense, but this one got me.

I had to resist the urge to write back a blistering email that would not only set the record straight but also squash him like a bug. My hands were still shaking when I calmed down a bit and typed out a few intense words of self-defense, telling him of my grief that day and that I had not given him a dirty look—that I spoke gently to him through my tears. I closed my email with the hopes that he would judge me more graciously.

Like I said, I don't generally respond to letters like his; I'm not sure I did the right thing in writing back. Perhaps my words didn't change anything. He could be just as convinced today as he was that day in front of the grocery store that I was unkind to him and that I'm stingy. But I've come to realize that the part that makes it hardest for me to forgive is my wounded pride—not my grief. I have to forgive people all the time who don't understand what it's like to experience catastrophic grief. But he judged something I feel good about. I think of myself as a giving person. To have him believe I'm stingy and unwilling to share with others in need hit my pride hard. Honestly, I want to keep rehearsing the incident. I want to keep telling the story because those who love me take up an offense on my behalf. But what good will that do? What else can I do but radically forgive him? To hold on to the hurt feelings and my sense of judgment and condemnation is to let bitterness gain a foothold in my soul. I have to release him and let him off the hook.

How about you? Have you struggled with forgiving a brother or a sister in Christ? Maybe you were knocked to your knees by the accusing, blaming, judging, or condemning words from a friend's mouth aimed at you or your husband. As we've already talked about, when hurt comes through someone we've served Jesus with, prayed with, poured out our hearts in trust and confidence to, walked through suffering with, laughed and played and worshiped with, that hurt feels like a complete betrayal. Maybe we expected better of fellow Christians, maybe we just never saw it coming, maybe we thought our mutual love for Jesus would protect us from the challenges of friendship.

Maybe your kids got caught in the cross fire. Maybe they're the ones who took the arrows and you're not just hurt; you're spitting mad. "How dare they treat my daughter like that?" Or "What made them think they could say such things about my kids?" This is dangerous territory for you as a parent. Nothing clouds our judgment quicker than feeling defensive about our beloved children. It takes the utmost wisdom to take a step back and evaluate tense situations that involve our kids so we can get a clear perspective. But let's say your perspective is clear and your children have been treated unfairly or unkindly and your emotions are running hot. Forgiving the offenders will take everything you've got.

Maybe rather than a personal wound inflicted on you or your family you're reeling from the revelation of someone's sinful behavior. Your fellow staff member had an affair . . . or got caught using porn . . . or has a drinking problem . . . or was discovered "borrowing" money from the church account. You're not only shocked but also disappointed and disillusioned and maybe even full of righteous anger at someone who should have known better.

But at the end of the day, we don't have many options. Holding grudges, keeping a record of wrongs, being guarded and distant with one another, refusing to let a hurt go, or waiting for the other person to apologize first are all responses that feel justified but will sabotage the unity and harmony God says *must* define his body, the church.

> How good and pleasant it is
>   when God's people live together in unity! (Ps. 133:1)

Through the peace that ties you together, do your best to maintain the unity that the Spirit gives. (Eph. 4:3 GW)

Do all that you can to live in peace with everyone. (Rom. 12:18 NLT)

The stakes are really high. Our unity in the church as characterized by radical forgiveness can bring someone to Christ or push them away from Christ. In fact, Jesus said in John 17:23 that when we are united together, people will know that God is real and that his love for them is real: "I in them and you in me—so that they may be brought to complete unity. Then the world will know that you sent me and have loved them even as you have loved me."

We have to look at the converse side of that verse and realize that when we are not unified, the world *doesn't* know that God is real and *doesn't* know that he loves them. Wow. This truth doesn't leave much room for our wounded pride—even if it's justifiable. François Fénelon wrote, "Your self-love is terribly touchy. No matter how slightly it is insulted, it screams, 'Murderer!'"[1] Most of us have a very difficult time giving up our claims to what we feel people owe us. But when we don't freely forgive, we love ourselves more than we love God—and more than we love the people who don't yet know God.

Again, Fénelon writes with wise counsel:

> Don't be so upset when things are said about you. Let the world talk; just seek to do the will of God. You will never be able to entirely satisfy people and it isn't worth the painful effort. Silent peace and sweet fellowship with God will repay you for every evil word spoken against you. Love your neighbor without expecting his friendship. People will come and go—let them do as they please. See only God. He is the One that afflicts or comforts you through people and circumstances. He does this for your benefit.[2]

Our *unity* in the church as characterized by radical *forgiveness* can bring someone to Christ or push them away from Christ.

I'm not sure how many books, sermons, speeches, songs, and dramas have been dedicated to forgiveness but probably thousands. I realize my few words aren't going to be the ones that shift the tide. All I can tell you is what I've learned in over forty years of ministry: radical forgiveness is the only way to survive criticism with your spirit intact.

⸺ Press In, Press On ⸺

Perhaps this conversation stirred up some strong emotions and memories for you as you reflect on your years in ministry. Maybe the faces of the people who betrayed you, hurt your kids, or damaged a congregation are fresh in your mind. Maybe you're in the middle of some fierce opposition right now and you've had the thought, *I can't do this anymore, God; I can't keep bearing this burden for you. I can't keep serving you knowing that people on all sides are jumping down our throats. I'm just too tired and hurt.*

I hear you, dear sister—I really do. This is the stuff that makes "sacred privilege" seem like a sick and cruel joke. This is the time for you to press in to your relationship with God. Remind yourself why you do what you do and who is the ultimate judge and evaluator of your life. Let him soften any bitter places that are taking root in your soul. Ask him to show you where to receive and embrace criticism, painful though it may be, and then give you the strength to make changes. Ask him to create a humble heart in you so that you can hold your ground without making power plays when you believe criticism is unjust or blown out of proportion. Ask for clarity to know when to call out unrighteousness and injustice and when to let him do his work in quieter ways. This is the time for you to cultivate a grateful soul and to do the hard work of forgiveness and restoration where possible, cognizant a watching world needs to see God's people living in harmony and unity so that they will know God loves them too.

11

Adopting an
Eternal Perspective

I will stick to Christ as a burr to cloth.

KATHARINA VON BORA,
wife of Martin Luther

*O*ver the course of a lifetime in ministry, you will experience dramatic changes—in yourself, your marriage, your family, your walk with God. You will encounter situations that stretch you beyond what you ever thought you could manage. You will learn how to expand your response to unpredictable circumstances and situations out of your control as you grow in flexibility, adaptability, and resilience. So much will change! Two things should remain stable and steady, though, if you want to last in ministry: your purpose and your perspective.

⟶ Align Your Purpose ⟵

What is your ultimate purpose in living every day? What motivates you to get out of bed each morning? Please don't reply too quickly and automatically give the dutiful response. We all know the answer is supposed to be something along the lines of, "My purpose is to please God." If we learn to actually *live* according to this principle, it will become the filter by which we evaluate everything that happens to us and will make us unshakable when the ground beneath us shifts.

My life purpose is summed up in 2 Corinthians 5:9: "So our aim is to please him always in everything we do, whether we are here in this body or away from this body and with him in heaven" (TLB).

There are a dozen reasons for me to get out of bed in the morning, from the profound to the mundane—love for my family, my job, my ministry, tasks to be accomplished, errands to run, appointments to keep—but the number one reason to throw the covers off is to say yes to God. Each new day allows me to affirm one more time that I understand I exist to please him and that he can do with me as he likes. I remind myself of my purpose throughout the day, otherwise I can get bent out of shape and forget why I'm even taking up space on this planet. I'm not here to have a flawlessly decorated home. I'm not here to make a great banana cake. I'm not here to write books or teach classes. I'm not here to be Rick's wife or my kids' mom. I'm here to please God. Do I bring him pleasure by loving well, using my gifts, fulfilling his calling? Absolutely. But at the core of it all is a surrendered heart that says yes no matter what.

Throughout this book, I've mentioned a few of the ministries I've been a part of through the years—church pianist, nursery coordinator, women's Bible study teacher, church membership class teacher, college ministry teacher, founder of the HIV&AIDS Initiative, volunteer in the mental health ministry. I mentioned them so quickly that you would never know that every time one of those ministry responsibilities changed, I grieved. Every time God asked me to let go of one area of ministry and take on another area of responsibility it was a wrestling match. Even if I was excited about the new thing he was asking me to do, there was a period in which I grieved the closing of a season of ministry I loved.

> Each new day allows me to *affirm* one more time that I understand I exist to *please* him and that he can do with me as he likes.

Once I accepted that I am an ordinary yet capable woman, I discovered God had given me the spiritual gift of teaching. I began leading our women's Bible study and loved it. I loved studying the Word, loved passing on the truths God was teaching me to the women of our church, loved seeing women come to Christ and then mature in their faith. But things changed when Amy was ten, Josh was seven, and Matthew was three. Matthew was—let's just say—an *active* little boy who needed a lot of my attention. He didn't play well by himself, which made it very challenging for me to study and prepare the weekly lessons. I discovered if I let him watch TV while I studied, I could prepare—with a minimum of interruptions—to teach women how to raise their children. I didn't spot the irony of putting my toddler in front of the TV for hours so I could teach other women how to raise their children. Hmm.

I'm embarrassed to say it took a while for me to see the disconnect, but one day it became crystal clear. I don't remember if something alerted me to the hypocrisy or not. All I remember is standing in the shower getting ready for a Bible study morning and hearing God say, "Kay, you need to let go of the Bible study; you have to give it away."

Have you had a conversation with God in which you *knew* he was telling you something but you pretended not to hear because if you acknowledged you heard him you'd have to do something about it? Sort of like those cell phone commercials in which the girl keeps saying, "I can't hear you, I can't hear you—must be bad reception" when her mother calls her. There is nothing wrong with the reception; she doesn't want to hear. That was me that day standing in the shower.

I started to argue with God. "Are you serious? You can't mean for me to give it up. I didn't ask for this ministry. *You* gave it to me! *You* gave me the gift of teaching. What am I supposed to do with it if not teach? Besides, women's lives are being changed. Why on earth would you ask me to give it up?" Next I tried to negotiate with the Lord. "What if I let Matthew watch TV for only two hours at a time instead of three hours? What if I alternate with another teacher so I have to prepare only two times a month? How about I find another mom to watch him so he's playing with other kids while I'm studying?" Those might all be reasonable adjustments for someone else, but God wasn't telling me to adjust. His words were crystal clear: "Give it away, Kay."

Amid the tears, I realized what I was really fighting—the fear that if I gave the Bible study away, someone else would do a better job. I was fearful that if at some point God gave me permission to resume teaching, the women would be disappointed I was coming back; they would have grown to love the new teacher more than me. Part of the issue was the need for me to be more engaged with my active little boy. But the issue wasn't as much about Matthew as it was about my tightly clenched fingers around not only a ministry I was afraid to entrust into God's hands but also my own self.

Eventually, I remembered my life purpose—to please God above all others, including myself. If God said to let the Bible study go, then I had to let it go. If the women loved the new teacher more than they loved me, then I had to be fine with that. If God never let me go back to teaching at all, he would show me something else. My purpose is settled and unshakable: to please him.

Have you experienced a wrestling match with God over what he's asking you to surrender? When you discover a special place to serve God that is fruitful and fulfilling, it's extremely difficult to let it go. When you fall in love with a church, it's painful to leave and turn it over to someone else. When it seems as though he's putting you on the shelf, it's hard to wait. Perhaps God has been whispering words to your spirit about change, letting go, moving on, and releasing, but you're doing what I did: pretending not to hear him talking to you. "Sorry, Lord; poor reception." Or you're arguing or trying to bargain with him. Maybe you hear him saying, "Yes, I've gifted you, but this is not the time and the season." Your purpose is to please him above yourself. You belong to God, and if he wants to take you from the head of the line and move you to the back of the line, that's okay. If he wants to remove

> My purpose is settled and *unshakeable*: to please him.

you from the line completely, that's okay. Your purpose is to please him—to be flexible, moldable, and movable in his hands. If your settled purpose is to please him, then you'll be able to adapt and adjust to the changes that come your way, confident that he has not forgotten you. Nailing down your purpose allows you to see in a new way situations you don't seem to have much control over or that don't make a lot of sense.

Adopt a New Perspective

Five years from now some of you who are reading this book will no longer be in ministry. Some of you will leave for other careers because God shifts your calling, and that's great. But some will leave because it all just got too hard and too painful. If you don't develop a perspective that can encompass situations that don't change, don't get any better, don't feel any different, or in which it's hard to have hope, you might eventually walk away. You might not walk away from God, but you might walk away from ministry. Or you'll stay in ministry but with a heart that has grown cold and barren toward God. I don't want you to stick it out with a numb heart, and I don't want you to leave because you didn't know how to see all that happens to you with an eternal perspective.

When you settle your purpose, a new perspective emerges, one that allows you to cope when the wheels fall off the bus—how to deal with the unavoidable loss, disappointment, betrayal, sorrow, failure, delay, or grief that comes to all of us. I hear from women like you every day who tell me about their dark places of struggle and hurt; some of these occur in the ministry and others occur in the intimate relationships we care about most.

As I said in chapter 10, wounds can happen as a result of ministry to fellow human beings who are far from perfect. We usually begin ministry with our arms open wide, ready to love a group of people and invite them to love us back. But then real life intrudes and the honeymoon period wears off. You opened your heart and your affections to your congregation only to be shut out, and it hurts. Our typical reaction is to close our arms bit by bit to protect ourselves from further hurt.

The apostle Paul experienced this with the Corinthian church. He shared his hurt feelings with them in 2 Corinthians 6:11–13: "We have spoken freely to you, Corinthians, and opened wide our hearts to you. We are not withholding our affection from you, but you are withholding yours from us. As a fair exchange—I speak as to my children—open wide your hearts also."

You've led people to Christ—loved them and discipled them. You've been there when their dog got sick, when someone in their family died, when their marriage was breaking up. You've been at all the happy times—the baby showers and wedding showers and graduation parties. You've spent hours with them. You've poured yourself into them only to have them decide they no longer want to be your friend or to be a part of your church. They might disagree with the church's vision or goals or the way the finances are being allotted. It could be a personality clash or a power struggle or a theological difference. At the end of the day, they think you and your husband are wrong and that anybody on the street corner could do a better job leading your church. They tell you they're leaving—or worse, they leave and don't tell you. Their departure causes a gigantic hole in your heart.

You might have experienced a tremendous hurt growing up, or in your marriage, or as a parent. Somebody in your life has hurt you. Maybe a whole bunch of somebodies have hurt you. Like the young man who molested me when I was very small, some of them meant to hurt you. But other people didn't mean to hurt you. In the course of the day-in and day-out interactions of relationships, it happened. Maybe they weren't there for you when you needed their love, encouragement, and support. Maybe they thought they were making good decisions, but their decisions had painful implications for you. Maybe the deepest hurts have come not from people but from the consequences of living in a world that is groaning, waiting for Christ's return. Perhaps you've suffered from physical ailments, disease, or chronic illness of body or mind, and you are weary from the fight.

As you read these words, it's possible there's a yawning well of pain in your heart. There's one in my heart too. But I'm determined not to walk away from God. I'm determined to look at even my deepest sorrow through the eternal perspective of God's point of view. The only way you and I will be able to stay strong until Jesus comes for us is to see everything through God's eyes. This eternal perspective doesn't just come automatically to everyone who becomes a Christian. It starts as a decision to live totally surrendered to God, but the initial decision must be fortified over years of knowing, loving, and trusting him.

The book of Genesis (chapters 37–50) records the story of Joseph and his family—a highly dysfunctional family, I might add. You know the story. Joseph is sold into slavery by his jealous brothers, who feel he is a narcissistic dreamer. He is taken to Egypt, where he eventually rises to prominence and becomes the second in command in Egypt. One day his brothers, who are facing famine in Israel, travel to Egypt seeking food. They don't realize their younger brother Joseph is in charge of food security and distribution—they don't even know he is still alive. As they kneel before this powerful man, they don't recognize him, but he recognizes them and begins a secret mission to be reunited with his father, Jacob. After Joseph reveals his identity, the brothers and Jacob move to Egypt, where Joseph cares for them.

> The only way you and I will be able to stay strong until *Jesus* comes for us is to see everything through God's *eyes*.

But eventually Jacob dies. Once their father is dead, the brothers fear Joseph will finally take revenge on them for selling him into slavery. They fall on their faces before him, affirming that they deserve to die for their treachery and brutality. They attempt to soften Joseph's heart toward them by relaying Jacob's dying wish for Joseph to forgive them.

With plenty of justification, Joseph could have punished them with the same cruelty they had inflicted on him years before. Instead, he gives one of the most moving declarations of an eternal perspective recorded in the Bible. In Genesis 50:20, Joseph looks at his brothers and says, "You meant to hurt me, but God turned your evil into good to save the lives of many people, which is being done" (NCV).

I cry every time I read Joseph's poignant, powerful words. He doesn't sugarcoat or minimize the injustice done to him. He doesn't shake it off with, "It was no big deal." He agrees with his brothers' acknowledgment that they sinned and wronged him and treated him very badly. "You meant to hurt me." We can reasonably expect that his next words will be, "In light of your admission of guilt for the terrible crime you committed against me, I sentence you to twenty-five years of hard labor" or "I banish you from my kingdom forever" or "I sentence you to death."

But that's not what Joseph says—and that's why this story reverberates through history.

Joseph says, "God turned your evil into good to save the lives of many people, which is being done." He understands God and faith in a way that is foreign to us. He explains what often feels unexplainable. He sees from God's point of view—he has an eternal perspective. He sees that God was at work in the evil and injustice done to him; he sees that God is turning evil on its head; he sees that the end result of betrayal, lies, abuse, abandonment, false accusations, and false imprisonment is millions of people surviving a brutal famine.

Joseph doesn't bury his suffering in a "leaders must be tough" mentality; he has the courage to admit he's been badly wounded. And then instead of exacting revenge, he forgives his brothers and speaks words of unbelievable faith in God's ability to bring good out of evil. This is a remarkable response to abuse and mistreatment. The story could end right here, and it would be a great story, worthy of being told and retold. But the story doesn't end with mere forgiveness of a relational debt owed. The last verse in the passage elevates the story to a remarkable height: "'You have nothing to fear. I will take care of you and your children.' So he reassured them with kind words that touched their hearts" (Gen. 50:21 GNT).

Not only did Joseph forgive his brothers and let them off the hook, but he also went beyond all reasonable expectations and *blessed* them. His vow to show mercy, kindness, compassion, and tenderness to the very ones who wounded him and left him for dead leaves me speechless. To be honest, there's a part of me that is defensive for Joseph—wasn't forgiveness enough? What else should this man who had been so badly mistreated have to do for his wretched brothers and their sorry offspring? How was this even possible? How did he manage to bless them—to offer what Dallas Willard defines as "the projection of good into the life of another."[1] Clearly, Joseph not only trusted God for the ability to speak and practice kindness and compassion to his tormentors but also trusted that God was working in the greatest pain and sorrow in his life.

This—*this*—is the eternal perspective that will take you through to the end. If you can begin to see from God's point of view, nothing will ever devastate you. Nothing.

We look at what has happened to us and start raising objections: "How can I ever let anyone see how badly that wounded me? How is it possible to radically forgive what has been done to me or my loved one? How can that wound ever be anything that brings good out of evil—how can it save the life of another person? And how can I possibly *bless* the very people who wounded me in the first place? How can I seek their good? It's simply not possible."

Every time I speak about being molested as a little girl, the sexual brokenness that resulted, and the ways God has healed me, there are women (and sometimes men) who whisper their own stories of molestation, rape, incest, and abuse. Often they tell me, "You're the first person I've ever told. If God could heal you and bring about restoration in your life, maybe there's hope for me too."

Hope is born; a life is saved.

When Rick and I talk about our marriage struggles, couples decide to try again. They conclude that if God can make a great marriage out of two of the most stubborn, immature, self-centered people he ever created, then maybe they too can build a marriage to last a lifetime.

Hope is born; a life is saved.

As I've begun to tell our story of how we are rebuilding our lives after the suicide of our beloved Matthew, other survivors have told me that our resilience in the face of one of life's most horrendous tragedies has led them to believe that they too will not only survive but also eventually thrive again.

> Cultivating an *eternal* perspective is what will keep you from walking away from *God* in the hard times.

Hope is born; a life is saved.

There's no doubt about it. The enemy of your soul meant it all for evil. He may have used fellow human beings to injure you, but behind what they did is what he was trying to do. He was trying to destroy you, kick the life out of you, make you walk away, make you decide you couldn't do this another day, that the cost was too high, that no call of God was worth the sacrifice you were being asked to make. You need to know in the core of who you are that God weeps with you and says, "I'm so sorry you were hurt; the wounds that broke your heart break mine as well. They have scarred you and drained the life out of you. But when you let me tend the wounds, I will use your scars for good—the saving of many lives."

Cultivating an eternal perspective is what will keep you from walking away from God in the hard times. There's one more guiding principle in John 21.

═══ Follow the W.I.T.T.Y. Principle ═══

Before Saddleback Church purchased land and built facilities, we really owned nothing. We rented buildings all over the Saddleback Valley—schools, banks, community centers— anything we could find to house our growing congregation. I knew when we planted Saddleback in our small condo that it would be like that for a while; I just didn't know it would take fifteen years before we owned a piece of land and built our first building. I thought in terms of five years. I told myself, *I can do this! I can handle all the moving around and the packing and unpacking of trailers full of folding chairs, nursery equipment, Sunday school materials, and audio equipment every Saturday and Sunday.* However, the glamour and excitement of church planting began to wear off as the inconvenience of temporary facilities took its toll. It wasn't fun to be a "pioneer" anymore. I longed for Saddleback to have a permanent home.

Through the years we attempted to buy property, and each time a potential deal came up, our faithful congregation cheerfully and sacrificially donated to the building fund. But each deal fell through—mostly because banks were reluctant to lend money to a church that owned nothing! Finally, after ten years, we were able to buy acreage in Orange County, California, and I thought the long wait was over. But . . . more drama was ahead. The county supervisors refused to grant us permission to build buildings because of some environmental concerns. So we finally had land, but we were unable to do a thing with it.

Rick worked tirelessly with the land search team from Saddleback, government officials, banks, and potential donors for years. He remained optimistic and upbeat no matter what setbacks and disappointments we incurred, and his optimism kept me afloat for a long time. But I'll never forget the day he came home from another meeting and said he had some really bad news. He told me the county was delaying our building plans indefinitely—after a two-year wait.

I'm not proud of what happened next; it wasn't pretty. I went ballistic. I screamed. I yelled at Rick, "You have been too nice to those people! You let *me* go down there to the county supervisors. I'll grab their ties, pull their faces two inches in front of my face, and yell until they give us our land! You just haven't done this the right way!"

Rick wisely backed away from the screaming mess I had become; there was nothing he could do or say to soothe my volcanic eruption.

Somehow I dragged myself into our home office and continued my hysterical meltdown, only this time the target was God. I bitterly hurled accusations at him. "You're playing a game with us! I don't get it. We have tried to do this all with integrity, with honesty. We've tried to use the best principles. We've tried to have faith. We have trusted you. We have believed you. We have done everything by the book. And this is our reward? This is how you treat us? Just tell me what game you're playing, God, because I am sick and tired of it."

Then I went from being bitter at God to being resentful and jealous of other pastors and their churches. With scathing sarcasm and rage, I reminded God that Bill Hybels and Willow Creek had land. Chuck Smith at Calvary Chapel in Costa Mesa had land and buildings. I told him that Adrian Rogers, then pastor of Bellevue Church in Nashville, had two hundred acres. And I said, "What does he need two hundred acres for? Take some of his land away from him and give it to us." I was being absurd. Completely irrational. And extremely self-centered.

After I'd thrown my hissy fit, lifted my fist to God's face, and basically accused him of loving everybody better than he loved us, the Lord did as he so often does: he sent me to his Word. "Go to John 21." In the stillness following my meltdown, I read this famous conversation between Jesus and Peter. Jesus asks Peter several times if he loves him. You remember it. Peter is a bit hurt that Jesus keeps asking him if he loves him and says repeatedly, "Yes! I love you!" Jesus responds each time, "Feed my sheep."

Most of the time we stop reading right there because the interchange between them has deep significance for love and service. The end of the conversation often gets left out. But that day it was the end of the conversation between Jesus and Peter that pierced my heart:

> "Very truly I tell you, when you were younger you dressed yourself and went where you wanted; but when you are old you will stretch out your hands, and someone else will dress you and lead you where you do not want to go." Jesus said this to indicate the kind of death by which Peter would glorify God. Then he said to him, "Follow me!"
>
> Peter turned and saw that the disciple whom Jesus loved was following them. (This was the one who had leaned back against Jesus at the supper and had said, "Lord, who is going to betray you?") When Peter saw him, he asked, "Lord, what about him?"

Jesus answered, "If I want him to remain alive until I return, what is that to you? You must follow me." (John 21:18–22)

The phrase "What is that to you?" was as powerful as a punch in the stomach, and I fell back in the chair, finally speechless. After I'd screamed, yelled, and accused God of every bad thing I could think of, he gently said, "Kay, what is that to you if I allow every church on the face of the earth to have land and buildings and Saddleback never does? Will you still follow me?"

That question took all the wind out of my argument. It obliterated all my accusations. It erased all my doubts and my hostility toward God. That question exposed my heart, and I clearly saw the ugliness and demandingness that had taken up residence in my core. Somehow a spirit of expectation had grown twisted roots and was yielding warped and damaged fruit. In essence, I had said to God, "I will serve you if you do what I want you to do. I will serve you if you give me what I think I deserve. I will serve you if you answer my prayers the way I think they need to be answered. I will serve you if you treat me the way I think I should be treated. I will serve you, I will follow you, I will feed your sheep. But, God, if you don't treat me fairly, then I don't want anything to do with you; I'm out of here."

My chastened, whispered heart answer to him that day was, "Yes, I will follow you no matter what. Even if every church on earth has land and buildings and Saddleback never does, I am yours. I will serve you until I die."

Jesus's response to your bitter, hostile, and angry accusations is exactly the same: "Dear one, what is that to you? If I allow this situation in your life to continue—the one that you think you can't handle another day, the one that you think is so unbearable, the one that you think is going to be the one that does you in—will you still follow me?" Or "If I don't answer your prayer the way you're begging for me to answer it—if those longings of your heart that are so deep and so much a part of who you are remain unfulfilled for the rest of your life—will you still follow me?" Or "If I answer her prayer differently than I answer yours and she receives what you have so passionately desired and you don't, will you still follow me?" Your answer also needs to be, "Yes, I will follow you even if *this* happens. Even if this doesn't happen. Even if you allow something in her life that you never allow in mine. Even if you allow something in my life that she never has to deal with. I will follow you. I will serve you until I die."

Of course, one moment of total surrender is never the end. Saying yes to God must become our habitual way of response to him—a thousand times a day, if necessary. One moment of surrender builds on top of another moment of surrender until our self-will is broken and is finally tempered like a wild stallion under the loving control of its master.

It was this momentous yes to God early in our ministry, followed by decades of yes after yes, that allowed my anguished heart to say on April 5, 2013, "Even if Matthew is not healed here on earth, I am yours. I will serve you until I die."

This is what it means to have an eternal perspective. This is what it means to believe that God is good and can be trusted with all the circumstances of your life and ministry. This is what will carry you through until the day Jesus comes for you. This is what will allow you to finish well.

12

Finishing Well

O glorious resurrection! O God of Abraham and
of all of our fathers, the believers of all the ages
have trusted on Thee and none of them have
hoped in vain. And now I fix my hope on Thee.

IDELETTE STORDER DE BURE CALVIN,
wife of John Calvin

A wise friend taught me to approach every situation with
the end in mind, to ask, "Where am I trying to go? What
is it I'm hoping to accomplish?" If I keep the end in mind at
all times, I will make choices, decisions, strategies, plans, and
actions based on what it will take to get there. In chapter 3, I
defined success in ministry as living with integrity, passion, and
a commitment to becoming like Christ; loving his church, his
Word, his world, and the people he's made; personal growth

in every area of life; gift development; and most of all finishing well. If finishing well is the end in mind, then knowing what it will take to get there is of prime importance.

If we use the race metaphor the apostle Paul seemed to love, it's easy to spot similarities between successfully completing a race and successfully completing a life in ministry. If you've ever watched a track event, you know getting off to a good start is what any runner wants, for it often determines the eventual winner. Running to the best of our ability, aware of where the other runners are yet with eyes focused on the finish line, is crucial. But what matters most is finishing in first place. In a physical race, there is only one winner, but in our spiritual race, everyone who runs gets a prize; what's at stake is the *quality* of the prize. In our spiritual race, we want to finish well—to know we've invested our time, energy, and passion in such a way that we will hear the Master's "well done." How can we know this side of eternity that we're running our race in a way that pleases God? What does it mean to finish well in a culture that elevates visible success?

> In a physical race, there is only one winner, but in our *spiritual* race, everyone who runs gets a prize; what's at stake is the *quality* of the *prize*.

—— The Cloud ——

Hebrews 11 and 12 contain the instructions for anyone seeking to live well and finish well. I'm not the first to find inspiration in these two chapters, but they have come to mean more to me since Matthew died, probably because his death has caused me to reevaluate what a life of faith entails. I've studied the men and women listed in Hebrews 11:1–40—God's "Hall of Famers"— "who through faith conquered kingdoms, administered justice, and gained what was promised; who shut the mouths of lions, quenched the fury of the flames, and escaped the edge of the sword; whose weakness was turned to strength; and who became powerful in battle and routed foreign armies. Women received back their dead, raised to life again" (vv. 33–35). These people—Abel, Enoch, Noah, Abraham, Isaac, Jacob, Joseph, Moses, Rahab, Gideon, Barak, Samson, Jephthah, David, Samuel, and the prophets—truly are heroes worthy of admiration and respect.

What stands out to me these days, though, is the smaller group—the nameless men and women listed simply as "others." These others were "tortured, refusing to be released so that they might gain an even better resurrection. Some faced jeers and flogging, and even chains and imprisonment. They were put to death by stoning; they were sawed in two; they were killed by the sword. They went about in sheepskins and goatskins, destitute, persecuted and mistreated—the world was not worthy of them. They wandered in deserts and mountains, living in caves and in holes in the ground" (11:35–38).

We know nothing else about them besides these meager words. Their lives are anonymous to us today—we can't put names or details to their stories—but God had a role for them to play that extended past their lifetimes.

The Bible says in Hebrews 12:1, "Therefore, since we are surrounded by such a great cloud of witnesses . . ." Who is in the great cloud of witnesses that surrounds us? Not only the great, named heroes of the faith but also the unnamed, unheralded others who did not build an ark, become the father of a nation, save Israel from famine, lead the children of Israel through the wilderness, see the walls of Jericho fall, or perform any of the other magnificent exploits that thrill us. Those unnamed brothers and sisters mean even more to me because they didn't see the victory . . . they didn't experience deliverance . . . they didn't get their miracle. In fact, far from receiving accolades or visible expressions of success, they had to keep believing and holding on to their faith under great duress—homelessness, torture, cruel punishment, poverty, persecution, and agonizing deaths. These others don't get as much attention in our A + B = C Christianity—you know, the kind of Christianity that insists that if you produce enough faith, you will be healed, you will be delivered, you will get your miracle. We don't usually put these people on the stage to give a testimony because their stories are not "success" stories. We'd much rather hear from someone like Moses or Gideon or even Rahab than from an unknown brother or sister whose hidden life of suffering makes us uncomfortable and challenges the accepted definition of what living by faith looks like.

I don't expect unbelievers to hold up the right measuring stick when it comes to defining a life of faith, but Christians certainly should. And according to the measuring stick of Hebrews 11,

> We're people of faith when we believe and miraculous things happen.
>
> We're people of faith when we believe and miraculous things don't happen.
>
> We're people of faith when we're named in the Hall of Fame.

We're people of faith when we're left nameless and invisible.

We're people of faith when we cross the finish line with arms held high in victory, sweaty and exhausted but on our feet.

We're people of faith when we walk carefully and deliberately across the finish line, slowed down by illness or effort.

We're people of faith when we crawl across the finish line with hands and knees bloody from what it cost us to run at all.

So what does it mean to live well and finish well?

One thing is certain: if we think living well and finishing well are only about receiving outward, external signs of God's approval, then we don't understand the high value God placed on the faith of the others in Hebrews 11 and their modern-day unknown brothers and sisters.

All of them pleased God because of their faith! But still they died without being given what had been promised. This was because God had something better in store for us. And he did not want them to reach the goal of their faith without us. (Heb. 11:39–40 CEV)

They, along with their more well-known fellow Hall of Fame members, did not receive what was promised in their lifetimes. The named and the unnamed died without the visible, complete fulfillment of their faith. Some of the more famous ones did gain earthly success and saw God at work in their lives, but it wasn't *all* that God had promised to them. They had to wait beyond their time here to reach the goal of their faith. If that was challenging for these people, how much more challenging was it for the others who didn't reach the goal of their faith here *and* greatly suffered as well?

Somehow these valiant men and women surround us from eternity's shores. Hebrews 12:1 definitely lets us know we're not alone in this race. They are in essence our cheering crowd. But not a cheering crowd of armchair spectators who have no idea of how treacherous and dark the race can get. They are a cheering crowd of champions . . . of *finishers*. I really don't know what they can see and how they help us, but at the very least, when we remember "this Christian way whereon I walk is no untried or uncharted road, but a road beaten hard by the footsteps of saints, apostles, prophets and martyrs,"[1] we can lift our heads, square our shoulders, and strengthen our resolve to stay on the path and keep running.

> One day you and I will *finish* the race, join that great cloud of witnesses, and be a part of those shouting *encouragement* to those still running the race.

One day you and I will finish the race, join that great cloud of witnesses, and be a part of those shouting encouragement to those still running the race. I get pretty excited to think about standing next to the people named in the Hall of Fame. I'm even more excited to stand next to the unnamed millions—if not billions—of men and women who lived and died ferociously hanging on to their faith against all the forces of hell. Make me worthy of them, Jesus.

Run Your Race for Jesus Alone

The passage in Hebrews goes on to tell us how to run the race: get rid of anything that slows us down, including sins that trip us up; patiently run our own individual race; and run with our eyes fixed on Jesus.

> Therefore, since we are surrounded by such a great cloud of witnesses, let us throw off everything that hinders and the sin that so easily entangles. And let us run with perseverance the race marked out for us, fixing our eyes on Jesus, the pioneer and perfecter of faith. For the joy set before him he endured the cross, scorning its shame, and sat down at the right hand of the throne of God. Consider him who endured such opposition from sinners, so that you will not grow weary and lose heart. (12:1–3)

We talked at length in chapter 4 about how God has uniquely formed and shaped you to run your own race. My friend Lyle, who is a marathon runner, tells me you have to run your race according to the body type God has given you. Your body is shaped in a certain way, and you have to run the race that only you can run.

Spiritually, you have no responsibility to run the race of another woman. Your only responsibility before God is to run the race he has marked out for you—the "particular race" (as The Living Bible puts it) he has called you to run. He has shaped you to run that race and that race alone. When we understand the futility of trying to run any race other than our own, it frees us from seeking the approval of others.

My sister, you cannot live your life for the approval of anyone but Jesus Christ. We simply can't measure up to all the expectations of the people in our churches; we'll never please everybody. Just about the time you get crowd A happy, crowd B is upset. If you jump to meet crowd B's desires, you risk making crowd A unhappy. And then crowds C and D chime in with their expectations, and before you know it, you're discouraged, beaten down, exhausted, resentful, and pulled in a thousand different directions. Our task is not to be people pleasers but Jesus pleasers and to run our race solely for him.

> Our *task* is not to be people pleasers but Jesus pleasers and to run our race *solely* for him.

Although I'm not a runner—at all—I resonate with the analogy here. Visualize this with me. You're running in a race, doing the best you know how to run well, avoid pits and roadblocks in the road, run efficiently and effectively, and stay focused on the finish line. But as you're running, you start to hear the whispers—sometimes the jeers—of the crowd. "Look at the way she runs! She runs like a duck! Where did she get those running shoes? They're terrible! Who told her she could finish this race?" If you turn to look at the jeering crowd, you're likely to stumble, lose your footing, and fall flat on your face.

Imagine another scenario. You're running your race, doing the best you can. You've trained and practiced, and you're giving it your full effort. And again from the crowd you hear voices, but this time they're voices of encouragement. You hear voices saying, "Good job! You're doing fantastic! Keep going! You are amazing!" If you turn your head to nod and wave in acknowledgment of their affirmations—"You know what? I'm pretty good!"—you can stumble, lose your footing, and fall flat on your face.

I recently watched four of my grandchildren participate in their school's annual jogathon. A microcosm of life unfolded right before my eyes. Cole, our first grader, was determined to run the entire time—not walk, not jog, but run. He started off at the front of the pack, giving it his all, but within a lap or two, he started slowing down. His mom and I yelled our support each time he rounded the track near us, but I realized we hadn't told him not to actually *look* at us as he ran by. He would hear our voices and turn his head to find us in the crowd, and several times I thought he was going down. The tangle of other small bodies around him running at a variety of speeds caused him to trip, but he managed to catch himself. It wouldn't have mattered if we were shouting support or hurling insults. If he had fallen while looking at us instead of the finish line, the result would have been the same.

The adoring crowd can be as big of a distraction as the jeering critics. It doesn't really matter whether discouragement or pride trips us up—either way, we're going to face-plant. The lesson is this: we must learn to ignore both the critics and the cheering crowd. Instead, we must focus on the finish line—or as the writer of Hebrews says, we must "fix our eyes on Jesus."

⸺ When You Can't See the Finish Line ⸺

If we want to finish well in life and ministry, we must believe and hold on to faith when others in the race oppose and criticize us, when we think we've run as far as we can and our strength has evaporated, when the obstacles in the way threaten to tank us, when the sun shines and when it's rainy, when we find ourselves momentarily off the track, and most of all when we can't see the finish line.

Myra Runyon competed in the fifteen-hundred-meter race for the United States in the 2000 Summer Olympics in Sydney,

Australia. At the time, Myra was thirty-one years old with macular degeneration, which means she could see only shapes and colors. She sensed when people were next to her as she ran. She had first competed in the Special Olympics, and this was her first chance to compete in the Olympics. I happened to catch her preliminary race, and she gave an interview. The newscaster asked her, "How do you do this? Describe what it's like to run a race you can't see."

She said, "You know, I come around the bend in those last few meters and I realize that I'm running toward a finish line that I can't see. It doesn't matter. I'm not slowing down for anything."

My life verse encapsulates what I'm trying to do here in however many years God gives me—I want to complete the task Jesus gave me and to finish my race.

> I consider my life worth nothing to me; my only aim is to finish the race and complete the task the Lord Jesus has given me—the task of testifying to the good news of God's grace. (Acts 20:24)

You and I are running toward a finish line we cannot see. If a woman competing in a sporting event will not slow down just because it's difficult, just because she can't see the end, then I'm not going to quit in my spiritual race either. We don't have to see the finish line. Myra said, "I can't see it but I know it's there." I don't see it—neither do you—but it's there. So run, sister, run, strengthened by the cloud of witnesses that surround our every step.

You and I are *running* toward a finish line we cannot *see*.

Don't let anything keep you from focusing on Jesus's face. Ignore the critics; paying attention to them will "kill" your spirit.

You're going to make it. It doesn't matter if you spring across the finish line or crawl; you're going to make it. Keep gazing into the eyes of the One who adores you, and run straight to Jesus.

I close with this prayer from my favorite prayer book, *A Diary of Private Prayer* by John Baillie:

> O Lord my God, I would kneel before Thee in lowly adoration ere I set out to face the tasks and interest of another day. I thank Thee for the blessed assurance that I shall not be called upon to face them alone or in my own strength, but shall at all times be accompanied by Thy presence and fortified by Thy grace. I thank Thee that through all our human life there runs the footprints of our Lord and Savior Jesus Christ, who for our sakes was made flesh and tasted all the changes of our mortal lot. I thank Thee for the many spiritual presences with which I shall today be surrounded as I go about my work. For the heavenly host above, for the saints who rest from their labours, for patriarchs, prophets and apostles, for the noble army of martyrs, for all holy and humble men of heart, for my own dear departed friends, especially _____ and _____. I bless and adore Thy great name. I rejoice, O God, that Thou hast called me to be a member of the Church of Christ. Let the consciousness of this holy fellowship follow me whithersoever I go, cheering me in loneliness, protecting me in company, strengthening me against temptation and encouraging me to all just and charitable deeds.[2]

ACKNOWLEDGMENTS

I want to thank four pastors' wives whose lives inspire me.

My mother, Bobbie Lawson Lewis, whose belief that "ministry is a privilege" was crucial in my formation as a woman, a Christian, and now a pastor's wife. She set the bar extremely high by the sacrificial way she loved Jesus, the Word of God, my pastor daddy, our family, and the congregations she served for more than fifty years. If ever there was an ideal pastor's wife, she was it. You were simply *the best*, Mama, and I can never thank you enough for living out your faith in front of me—imperfectly, of course, but sincerely, deeply, and faithfully. I wanted to be in full-time ministry because of you and Dad. Alzheimer's disease may be robbing you of your memory, but I can still see *you*. I adore you!

My mother-in-love, Dorothy Armstrong Warren, whose generous spirit taught me all I ever needed to know about having an open heart and an open home in life and in ministry, willingly gave herself to the small churches she served for more than fifty years with Rick's dad, Jimmy. Having welcomed me into her embrace the first time she met me, she kept our sweet relationship going by calling me her daughter-in-love until her death in 1996. I love you and miss you, Dot, and can't wait to jump into your warm, squishy hug again!

My sister-in-love, Chaundel Warren Holladay, is the sister I longed for as a little girl. We bonded instantly when we met at sixteen and nineteen respectively, and nothing can ever shake our devotion to each other. We are polar opposites in personality (she out-Tiggers Rick), and she has a brain the size of Montana (mine could fit in my backyard). She has stayed by my side in joy and in sorrow and is fiercely loyal to me. As a pastor's wife, she continues the model of openness and hospitality she learned from her mom and dad, and the women married to Saddleback pastors receive the tenderest care from her. I love you dearly, sweet sister of my heart.

Most of all, I want to thank my daughter, Amy Warren Hilliker, who lives with a radical passion for Jesus, his Word, his church in general, and Saddleback Church specifically. It would be easy for her to toss out everything she experienced growing up under her mom and dad—after all, we're pretty messy and made a lot of mistakes—yet she digs in her heels and works for the spiritual health and vitality of this place. She is the bravest woman I know, courageously raising three children with Lyme disease while battling it herself. My girl teaches me every day about sacrifice, commitment, and obedience when it's hard; hope for better days; joy in the moment; and how to never give up. I love you, darling Amy!

To Josh: You are a man who follows hard after Jesus, even when it isn't easy, fun, or feels good. I love the man you are, my son, and the man you're becoming. Thank you for the unbelievable support you give to me every day—particularly as I write. You are the best literary agent I could ask for, always looking out for me, shepherding book projects from start to finish. I know I'm in good hands when you're involved! Love you forever . . .

And to Rick: I met you when you were seventeen. You were tall and skinny and had curly blond hair, John Lennon glasses, pimples, and long arms and legs. You were also loud—extremely loud—funny, a good guitar player, and did a fabulous Billy Graham impersonation. You had this really, really outgoing personality. You also were crazy for Jesus—embarrassingly bold in your witness and in your desire to see people come to know Christ. No one who knew you then can forget your white, beat-up Chevy van that was covered with Jesus bumper stickers (I mean *covered*). They also can't forget about the casket (where did you get that by the way?) that you and Danny Daniels strapped to the top of your van and popped out of as an evangelism tool. Or the street witnessing that included shouting out "Jesus loves you more than your boyfriend does" to startled couples innocently walking down the street, which horrified the shy, introverted adolescent I was.

From there, you toned it down a bit as you matured into your twenties. Good thing too, because I simply *couldn't* marry a man who popped out of a coffin on a regular basis or hang out with a guy who wore a Santa costume into a bar to witness to drunks on Christmas. Your passion for Jesus and for evangelism continued unabated, but thankfully, you learned more socially appropriate ways to share your faith. You even chose to go to seminary after college graduation, a decision you seriously pondered because, after all, Jesus didn't go to seminary and the apostle Paul didn't go to seminary. If they didn't need to "waste" time in the stuffy, establishment-oriented, ivory tower of academia, why did you? People were dying and going to hell every day. Seminary seemed like a pointless exercise in what you "should" do rather than what fiery young preachers were called to do, which was preach repentance!

You actually ate seminary up with a spoon—you had astonishingly (to you) well-informed and godly professors who stimulated your zeal and equipped you biblically—and it was there that the dream of planting a church was born. What happened to you in seminary radically affected the course of our lives, and I'm forever grateful. You caught a vision of reaching people turned off by and alienated from traditional churches, and while we initially thought we would be missionaries in another land, God asked us to become "missionaries" to the uninterested, disenfranchised yuppies of Southern California. It was God-humor, since we were pretty much country bumpkins, as different as night and day from the people we felt called to pastor in sophisticated, affluent Orange County, California. And yet God's call was clear and unambiguous, and so we headed west from Fort Worth, Texas, back to our California roots—you, me, and our four-month-old baby girl, Amy Rebecca, with no building, no members, and no money. You instantly went from jeans, Pendleton shirts, and desert boots to a patterned three-piece suit with a starched white shirt and tie. Like I said, God-humor.

And now we're approaching our fortieth anniversary in the church—Saddleback Valley Community Church—we started in the living room of our rented condominium in 1980. How is that possible? How did nearly four decades go by so quickly?

Somewhere along the way I blinked. One glance in the mirror at either of us, though, and it's clear that nearly four decades have passed. I think your look has changed more radically than mine. I've always been Miss Prim and Proper, but you've gone from a three-piece suit to gaudy Hawaiian shirts; then to Dockers and boat shoes; then to T-shirts, jeans, and Converse shoes. Now the once gangly, long-haired Jesus freak sports short blond hair, stylish glasses, nice jeans, and plaid shirts (hurry up next trend; plaid shirts are getting old) on a more robust frame!

Through it all—and I mean *all*—you've been the source of both my deepest love and my greatest frustration (we are polar opposites remember). I knew when I met you that you were truly unique, and forty-five years later you remain the most unique person I know. You are such a bundle of strengths and weaknesses, and to stand by your side and watch God slowly untangle the knots and use you to expand his kingdom has been the greatest honor I've had. To start a family with you, to start Saddleback Church with you, to dream with you, to plan with you, to sacrifice with you, to create with you, to grow with you, to fight with you, to forgive with you, to laugh and cry with you, to mourn with you, to endure with you, to hope with you . . . who could ask for more?

You, my dearest husband, have taught me more about caring for a congregation than any class I've ever taken, any book I've ever read, any conference I've ever attended, or any pastor I've ever known. To be your wife; raise Amy, Josh, and Matthew; and serve Jesus hand in hand with you at Saddleback Church is all I could ever have wanted for this lifetime.

Thank you for believing in me when I didn't see gifts and abilities in myself; for pushing me forward *way* outside of my comfort zone; for opening up opportunities for me to serve and minister at Saddleback; for knocking down barriers and obstacles you felt weren't right; for adjusting yourself to accommodate God's ministry through me; and for being humble enough to seek my opinion and thoughts and to learn from me. Thank you for being comfortable with me telling our story in its entirety—the good, the bad, and the ugly. You are such a good man, Rick Warren, and I am positively giddy that you are mine!

My team at Acts of Mercy is made up of the most loving and sacrificial women who serve Jesus wholeheartedly. Their passion for people living with mental illness is a constant source of inspiration to me. Joy, Jeanne, Ashley, Lauren, Laura, and Nancy—I can't thank you enough for the ways you supported me in this writing process. Thanks for the prayers, research, middle-of-the-afternoon Bundt cake breaks, laughing at my stupid jokes, putting up with my drama, and telling me I could do this on the days I thought it was impossible. Your friendship and partnership in ministry mean the world to me.

No author can do it alone, and I'm no exception. Many thanks to the caring and skilled folks at Revell—especially to Andrea Doering and Twila Bennett. You smooth the way for me, calm my anxious fears, offer the most helpful advice, and turn my vision into reality! It's always a pleasure to work together on a book project.

NOTES

Chapter 2: Sharing the Dream

1. Cambridge Academic Content Dictionary (Cambridge, England: Cambridge University Press, 2008).

Chapter 4: Adapting to Change

1. C. S. Lewis, *The Lion, The Witch and the Wardrobe* (New York: Harper-Collins, 2008), 80.

Chapter 5: Helping Your Children Survive and Thrive

1. David Seamands, *Healing for Damaged Emotions* (Colorado Springs: David C. Cook, 1981), 32-33.

2. Commencement address, Bates College, Lewiston, ME, June 4, 2001.

3. Henri Nouwen, *Here and Now* (New York: Crossroad, 1994), 143.

Chapter 6: Sharing Your Life

1. Paul David Tripp, *Whiter Than Snow: Meditations on Sin and Mercy* (Wheaton: Crossway, 2008), 32.

2. Edward Bratcher, *The Walk-on-Water Syndrome* (Nashville: W Publishing, 1984).

3. Oswald Chambers, *My Utmost for His Highest* (New York: Dodd, Mead & Co., 1935), day 67.

4. Bratcher, *The Walk-on-Water Syndrome*, 40.

5. Larry Crabb, *Connecting* (Nashville: Thomas Nelson, 1997), 147.

Chapter 7: Taking Care of Yourself

1. Gail McDonald, *High Call, High Privilege* (Peabody, MA: Hendrickson, 1998), 2.

2. Charles Swindoll, *Growing Strong in the Seasons of Life* (Grand Rapids: Zondervan, 1983), 433.

3. Gabe Lyons, "A Candid Interview with Eugene Peterson," ChurchLeaders.com.

4. Peter Scazzero, *Emotionally Healthy Spirituality* (Nashville: Thomas Nelson, 2006), 163.

Chapter 8: Valuing Seasons and Moments

1. Gabe Lyons, "A Candid Interview with Eugene Peterson," ChurchLeaders.com.

2. John Gill, *John Gill's Exposition of the Entire Bible* (Seattle: Amazon Digital Services, 2012).

3. Bob Benson, *Laughter in the Walls* (Nashville: Thomas Nelson, 1990).

4. Elisabeth Elliot, *Through Gates of Splendor* (Wheaton: Tyndale, 1981), 20.

Chapter 9: Protecting Your Private Life

1. Edith Schaeffer, *What Is a Family?* (Grand Rapids: Revell, 1975), 183.

2. François Fénelon, *The Seeking Heart* (Jacksonville, FL: SeedSowers, 1992), 53.

3. Michael O'Donnell, *Help! I'm a Pastor's Wife* (Nashville: Thomas Nelson, 1992), 48.

Chapter 10: Dealing with Criticism

1. François Fénelon, *The Seeking Heart* (Jacksonville, FL: SeedSowers, 1992), 79.

2. Ibid., 49.

Chapter 11: Adopting an Eternal Perspective

1. Dallas Willard, *Living in Christ's Presence* (Downers Grove, IL: InterVarsity, 2014).

Chapter 12: Finishing Well

1. John Baillie, *A Diary of Private Prayer* (New York: Scribner, 2014), 25.

2. Ibid., 93.

RECOMMENDED RESOURCES

Book Recommendations

Anxiety/Stress/Burnout

Hart, Dr. Archibald D. *Adrenaline and Stress: The Exciting New Breakthrough That Helps You Overcome Stress Damage*. Dallas: World Publishing, 1995.

Scazzero, Peter. *The Emotionally Healthy Leader: How Transforming Your Inner Life Will Deeply Transform Your Church, Team, and the World*. Grand Rapids: Zondervan, 2015.

———. *Emotionally Healthy Spirituality: It's Impossible to Be Spiritually Mature, While Remaining Emotionally Immature*. Grand Rapids: Zondervan, 2014.

Simpson, Amy. *Anxious: Choosing Faith in a World of Worry*. Downers Grove, IL: InterVarsity, 2014.

Depression

Marchenko, Gillian. *Still Life: A Memoir of Living Fully with Depression*. Downers Grove, IL: InterVarsity, 2016.

Sheffield, Anne. *How You Can Survive When They're Depressed: Living and Coping with Depression Fallout*. New York: Three Rivers Press, 1998.

Strauss, Claudia J. *Talking to Depression: Simple Ways to Connect When Someone in Your Life Is Depressed*. New York: New American Library, 2004.

General Book Recommendations

Baker, John. *Life's Healing Choices: Freedom from Your Hurts, Hangups, and Habits*. New York: Howard Books, 2007.

Hannaford, Chuck. *Picking Up the Pieces Handbook: Creating a Dynamic Soul-Care Ministry in Your Church*. Nashville: Lifeway Christian Resources, 2009.

London, H. B., and Neil Wiseman. *Married to a Pastor: How to Stay Happily Married in the Ministry*. Grand Rapids: Baker Books, 1999.

Warren, Rick, DMin, Mark Hyman, MD, and Daniel Amen, MD. *The Daniel Plan: 40 Days to a Healthier Life*. Grand Rapids: Zondervan, 2013.

Yerkovich, Milan and Kay. *How We Love: Discover Your Love Style, Enhance Your Marriage*. Colorado Springs: Waterbrook Press, 2008.

Grief

Grippo, Daniel. *When Mom or Dad Dies: A Book of Comfort for Kids*. St. Meinrad: Abbey Press, 2008.

Guthrie, David, and Nancy Guthrie. *When Your Family's Lost a Loved One: Finding Hope Together*. Colorado Springs: Focus on the Family, 2008.

Guthrie, Nancy. *Hearing Jesus Speak into Your Sorrow*. Carol Stream, IL: Tyndale Momentum, 2009.

Haugk, Kenneth C., PhD. *Don't Sing Songs to a Heavy Heart: How to Relate to Those Who Are Suffering*. St. Louis: Stephen Ministries, 2004.

Hsu, Albert Y. *Grieving a Suicide: A Loved One's Search for Comfort, Answers & Hope*. Downers Grove, IL: InterVarsity, 2002.

Lewis, C. S. *A Grief Observed*. Nashville: HarperOne, 2001.

Nouwen, Henri J. M. *Turn My Mourning into Dancing: Finding Hope in Hard Times*. Nashville: W Publishing, 2001.

Sittser, Jerry. *A Grace Disguised: How the Soul Grows through Loss*. Grand Rapids: Zondervan, 2004.

Weems, Ann. *Psalms of Lament*. Louisville: Westminster John Knox, 1995.

Mental Health

Amador, Xavier, PhD. *I Am Not Sick, I Don't Need Help! How to Help Someone with Mental Illness Accept Treatment*. Peconic, NY: Vida Press, 2011.

Amen, Daniel G., MD. *Change Your Brain, Change Your Life: The Breakthrough Program for Conquering Anxiety, Depression, Obsessiveness, Lack of Focus, and Memory Problems*. New York: Harmony Books, 2015.

Beach, Shelly, and Wanda Sanchez. *Love Letters from the Edge: Meditations for Those Struggling with Brokenness, Trauma, and the Pain of Life*. Grand Rapids: Kregel, 2014.

Rennebohm, Craig, and David Paul. *The Companionship Series (#1: Mental Health Ministry: An Introduction, #2: The Way of Companionship: Welcoming the Stranger, and #3: Organizing a Congregational Mental Health Team)*. Seattle: Mental Health Chaplaincy, 2012.

Simpson, Amy. *Troubled Minds: Mental Illness and the Church's Mission*. Downers Grove, IL: InterVarsity, 2013.

Stanford, Matthew S., PhD. *Grace for the Afflicted: A Clinical and Biblical Perspective on Mental Illness*. Downers Grove, IL: InterVarsity, 2008.

Swinton, John. *Resurrecting the Person: Friendship and the Care of People with Mental Health Problems*. Nashville: Abingdon, 2000.

Mental Health: Children and Teens

Purvis, Karyn B., PhD, David R. Cross, PhD, and Wendy Lyons Sunshine. *The Connected Child: Bring Hope and Healing to Your Adoptive Family*. New York: McGraw-Hill Education, 2007.

Purvis, Karyn B., PhD, and Elizabeth Styffe. *The Connection: Where Hearts Meet Small Group Study*. DVD series.

Siegl, Daniel J., MD, and Tina Payne Bryson, PhD. *The Whole Brain Child: 12 Revolutionary Strategies to Nurture Your Child's Developing Mind*. New York: Bantam Books, 2012.

Yerkovich, Milan and Kay. *How We Love Our Kids: The Five Love Styles of Parenting*. Colorado Springs: Waterbrook Press, 2011.

Pastors' Wives and Kids

Buckingham, Michele. *Help! I'm a Pastor's Wife*. Nashville: Thomas Nelson, 1992.

Dobson, Lorna. *I'm More Than the Pastor's Wife: Authentic Living in a Fishbowl World*. Grand Rapids: Zondervan, 2003.

Dugan, Lynne. *Heart to Heart with Pastors' Wives: Twelve Women Share the Wisdom They've Gained as Partners in Ministry*. Grand Rapids: Baker Books, 1994.

Floyd, Jeana. *10 Things Every Minister's Wife Needs to Know*. Green Forest, AR: New Leaf Press, 2010.

Lee, Cameron. *Life in a Glass House: The Minister's Family in Its Unique Social Context*. Pasadena: Fuller Seminary Press, 2006.

———. *PK: Helping Pastors' Kids through Their Identity Crisis*. Grand Rapids: Zondervan, 1992.

London, H. B., and Neil Wiseman. *Married to a Pastor's Wife: A Read-Together, Write-Together Book to Help Pastoral Couples Survive Ministry Risks*. Wheaton: Victor Books, 1995.

———. *Pastors at Greater Risk: Real Help for Pastors from Pastors Who've Been There*. Grand Rapids: Baker Books, 2003.

MacDonald, Gail. *High Call, High Privilege: A Pastor's Wife Speaks to Every Woman in a Place of Responsibility*. Peabody, MA: Hendrickson, 1998.

Ray, Charles, and Susannah Spurgeon. *Susannah Spurgeon: Free Grace and Dying Love*. Edinburgh: Banner of Truth, 2006.

Scazzero, Geri. *I Quit! Stop Pretending Everything Is Fine and Change Your Life*. Grand Rapids: Zondervan, 2011.

Wilhite, Lori, and Brandi Wilson. *Leading and Loving It: Encouragement for Pastors' Wives and Women in Leadership*. New York: FaithWords, 2013.

Talking to Your Kids about Sex

Bimler, Rich. *Sex and the New You*. St. Louis: Concordia Publishing, 2015.

Burns, Jim. *The Purity Code: God's Plan for Sex and Your Body*. Minneapolis: Bethany House Publishers, 2008.

Buth, Lenore. *How to Talk Confidently with Your Child about Sex: For Parents (Learning about Sex)*. St. Louis: Concordia Publishing, 2015.

Chu, Jeff. *Does Jesus Really Love Me?: A Gay Christian's Pilgrimage in Search of God in America*. New York: Harper, 2014.

McKee, Jonathan. *More Than Just the Talk: Becoming Your Kids' Go-To Person about Sex*. Minneapolis: Bethany House Publishers, 2015.

―――. *Sex Matters*. Minneapolis: Bethany House Publishers, 2015.

Penner, Dr. Clifford and Joyce. *Sex Facts for the Family*. Nashville: W Publishing, 1992.

Sprinkle, Preston. *Living in a Gray World: A Christian Teen's Guide to Understanding Homosexuality*. Grand Rapids: Zondervan, 2015.

Stanley, Andy. *The New Rules for Love, Sex, and Dating*. Grand Rapids: Zondervan, 2015.

Recommended Websites and Blogs

Clergy Finances and Taxes

clergysupport.com

clergytax.com

clergytaxnet.com

guidestone.org

Ministry Research

Bible.org

Biblegateway.com

CCEL.org

crosswalk.com

equippedforliving.org

theopedia.com

Pastors' Wives

apreacherswife.com

clutchtalk.blogspot.com

justbetweenus.org

kaywarren.com

leadingandlovingit.com

pastorspouses.com

Clergy Retreat Centers

Blessing Ranch Ministries | blessingranch.org

The mission of Blessing Ranch Ministries is "to restore and renew Christian leaders and their families for effective Kingdom service." The goal of this incredibly effective, essential ministry is and always has been emotional and spiritual inner reengineering and personal growth resulting in restoration and renewal of the leader.

Broom Tree Ministries | broomtreeministries.org

The mission of Broom Tree Ministries is to provide a gracious environment, secluded and private, protected with prayer, to which Christian leaders and their spouses can retreat from frantic schedules and become intimate with God so that he can refresh, refocus, restore, encourage, energize, and equip them for the task to which he has called them.

The Cottage on Coronado Island | coronadocottage.org

Enjoy the beautiful seascape of Coronado Island, a year-round resort area. Couples come to the cottage seeking intensive therapy for a crisis in marriage or ministry. Individuals come seeking personal renewal through multiple therapy session for interpersonal conflict, stress, burnout, career transitions, and spiritual direction.

Cozy Bear Cabins | cozybearcabins.com

Cozy Bear Cabins is a group of three distinctive cabins located in the Smoky Mountain National Park area. If you like to be close to the action and excitement of Pigeon Forge and Gatlinburg, Tennessee, then Cozy Bear fits the bill. Located in a luxury resort community setting, Cozy Bear is the perfect family cabin with a mountain theme.

Deer Ridge Ministries | drmretreats.org

Deer Ridge Ministries was formed to encourage pastors in full-time ministry. They provide, by faith, excellent retreat facilities where pastors and spouses can rest and enjoy the presence of God without having to worry about any financial obligation. God has called Deer Ridge Ministries to provide a needed refuge for pastors and their spouses. They are here to provide a place of peace, refreshment, and rest for body and soul at no cost to their guests.

Fairhaven Retreat Center | fairhavenministries.net

Pastors and missionaries often need an affordable place away from the demands of their ministry where they can rest and relax. The beautiful facilities and serenity of the natural surroundings, combined with the absence of telephones, televisions, or schedules, make Fairhaven the ideal place for a getaway. Individuals, couples, and families can all enjoy a personal retreat at Fairhaven.

Marble Retreat | marbleretreat.org

Marble Retreat was born out of the conviction that clergy and others in Christian service have extreme job demands that can frequently result in symptoms of depression, anxiety, frustration, discouragement, and burnout. Worse still and because of their position, they find it difficult to seek help. The mission of Marble Retreat is to help bring healing, hope, and restoration to those in vocational Christian ministry and the church at large through Christ-centered, brief, intensive counseling.

Mountain Learning Center | pastor-care.com

The MLC is located in June Lake, California, beneath the awe-inspiring Sierra Nevada Mountain Range. In the context of an alpine, mountainous retreat environment, Christ-centered and biblically relevant principles of relationships with God, self, and others are embraced and developed through the vehicle of counseling from a spiritual formation perspective.

Rocky Mountain Renewal | rockymountainrenewal.org

This ministry provides vacation homes for full-time evangelical pastors and missionaries and their families. Their goal is to provide a place of refreshment and relaxation for those who are in so much need of rest. (Requires a username; phone: 970-259-7778 or email: info@rockymountainrenewal.org)

Clergy Counseling and Treatment Centers

Barnabas Ministries | barnabasmin.org
Charis Foundation | charisfoundation.com
Clergy Recovery | clergyrecovery.com
Focus on the Family | thrivingpastor.com

Kay Warren cofounded Saddleback Church with her husband, Rick Warren, in Lake Forest, California. She is a passionate Bible teacher and respected advocate for those living with mental illness, HIV, and for orphaned and vulnerable children. She founded Saddleback's HIV&AIDS Initiative. Kay is the author of *Choose Joy: Because Happiness Isn't Enough* and *Say Yes to God* and coauthor of *Foundations*, the popular systematic theology course used by churches worldwide. Her children are Amy and Josh, and Matthew who is in heaven, and she has five grandchildren, Kaylie, Cassidy, Caleb, Cole, and Claire. Learn more at www.kaywarren.com and follow her on Facebook (Kay Warren) and on Twitter (@KayWarren1).

From bestselling author

Kay Warren

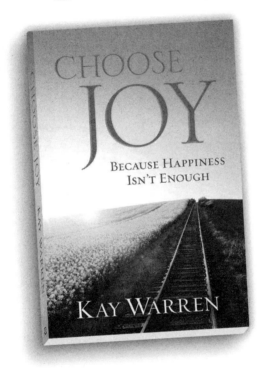

In *Choose Joy*, acclaimed author and Christian leader Kay Warren explains the path to experiencing soul-satisfying joy no matter what you're going through. Joy is deeper than happiness, lasts longer than excitement, and is more satisfying than pleasure and thrills. Joy is richer. Fuller. And it's *far more accessible* than you've thought.

Perfect *for* Small Groups!

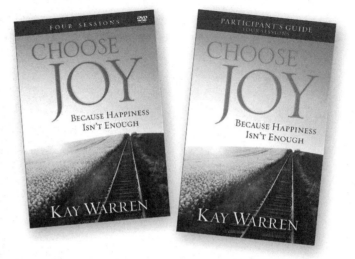

In this *Choose Joy* four-session video-based study, Kay Warren encourages you to examine your beliefs and choices about happiness and joy. In her honest and engaging style, she will challenge you to consider new ways of thinking, feeling, and acting that allow joy to take root and grow, even in the darkest times. In the *Choose Joy* participant's guide, small group questions are provided to enhance discussion, meditation, and personal application.

Choose Joy DVD Curriculum & Participant's Guide Include:

Session One: Jesus, Man of Joy
Session Two: Joy Is a Conviction of My Mind
Session Three: Joy Is an Attitude of My Heart
Session Four: Joy Is a Choice of My Behavior

Available at
KayWarren.com or Wherever Resources Are Sold

A 30-DAY
JOURNEY OF FAITH

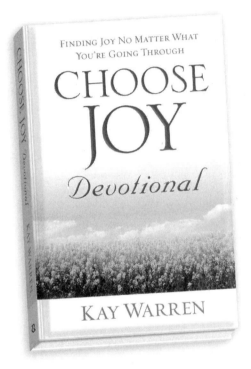

Joy is a daily choice. With deep compassion, Kay offers thirty devotions based on the life-giving principles of her book *Choose Joy*. Each devotion begins with an encouraging Scripture, followed by Kay's wise words, and ends with a short prayer.

Revell

a division of Baker Publishing Group
www.RevellBooks.com

Available wherever books and ebooks are sold.

STAY CONNECTED WITH

Visit KayWarren.com to connect with Kay, sign up for the free email devotions, and order other books and curriculum by Kay.

In addition, you will find information and resources about the passions of Kay's heart: mental health, suicide prevention, orphans and vulnerable children, HIV/AIDS, the PEACE Plan, and encouragement for pastors' wives.

	Kay Warren		KayWarren1
	KayWarren75		KayWarren1

Visit **KayWarren.com**, email Kay@KayWarren.com, or call the office of Kay Warren at (949) 609-8552.